ITALIAN DRAWINGS
FROM THE BICK COLLECTION

Selections from the Collection of
Esther S. and Malcolm W. Bick

ITALIAN DRAWINGS

Hopkins Center · Dartmouth College

HANOVER · NEW HAMPSHIRE

1971

HOPKINS CENTER ART GALLERIES
Dartmouth College, Hanover, New Hampshire
April 2 – April 25, 1971

THE CURRIER GALLERY OF ART
Manchester, New Hampshire
July 24 – August 29, 1971

BOWDOIN COLLEGE MUSEUM OF ART
Brunswick, Maine
September 16 – October 24, 1971

WADSWORTH ATHENEUM
Hartford, Connecticut
January 4 – February 14, 1972

JOHN AND MABLE RINGLING MUSEUM OF ART
Sarasota, Florida
March 3 – March 31, 1972

JEWETT ARTS CENTER
Wellesley College, Wellesley, Massachusetts
April 15 – June 11, 1972

EDITED BY

FRANKLIN W. ROBINSON AND JOHN T. PAOLETTI

COVER: Perino del Vaga, no. 4
TITLE PAGE: Palma il Giovane, no. 12, detail

Acknowledgments

TO a great degree, Italian art has, until the last century, been the heart of the Western tradition, and Italian drawings have been its most intimate expression. It is, then, with great pride that the Hopkins Center Art Galleries at Dartmouth College presents to a wide public a selection from the major collection of Italian drawings formed by Esther S. and Malcolm W. Bick. We are indeed grateful to the collectors for their generosity in sharing their drawings with our students for so many months and with the public at large for over a year. Their "Note on Collecting" in this catalogue is ample testimony to their love of art and, even more important, artists; we might just add that it is interesting that one member of this collecting team has a background in the theatre, while the other is an eye surgeon, surely a perfect combination for responding to the visual drama of Italian art.

This catalogue has been prepared as an undergraduate seminar under the supervision of Professors Franklin W. Robinson and John T. Paoletti of the Dartmouth Art Department; seminars centered around an exhibition and a catalogue have become a tradition at Dartmouth and we hope that their value for the participating students will be matched by the interest of the catalogue for the lay and scholarly public. Professors Robinson and Paoletti, who have edited the catalogue and prepared the exhibition itinerary, would like to thank not only the students in the seminar but also the collectors and museum officials who were especially helpful to them in their trips with the students during the course. Among these are John Nicholas Brown, Marjory B. Cohn, Wolfgang Freitag, Linda Gillies, Anne-Marie Logan, Susan Reed, Felice Stampfle, and Eunice Williams; a special debt of thanks must go to the generosity and hospitality of Janós Scholz.

Many scholars have seen the Bicks' collection and made valuable comments on it or have been kind enough to respond to our letters asking for opinions or information; we are especially grateful to Leonard Baskin, Nathan Chaikin, Miles Chappell, Iris Cheney, Bernice Davidson, Charles Dempsey, Herbert

Feist, Ivan Fenyö, Sidney Freedberg, Alan Gaylord, Michael Jaffé, George Knox, Norman Leitman, Christopher Lloyd, J. C. D. Marshall, Mary Newcome, Konrad Oberhuber, Stephen Ostrow, Philip Pouncey, Eckhard Schaar, Janós Scholz, Wolfgang Stechow, and P. A. Tomory.

We are also grateful to the museums who are participating in this project and, particularly, David Brooke, Curtis Coley, Peter Marlow, Harry Schnabel, and Richard West.

Mrs. Helen P. Weigle generously typed and edited most of the correspondence and catalogue material; Hyman Edelstein took the excellent photographs used by the seminar for various study purposes. Roderick Stinehour has been responsible for the design of the catalogue.

The staff of Hopkins Center Art Galleries must also be thanked: Evelyn Landry, for typing the final draft of the catalogue, Barbara Horton, who has handled the complicated problems of the transportation of the drawings, and Winfred Derosie, who has been responsible for packing and handling the works.

TRUMAN H. BRACKETT, JR.
Director, Hopkins Center Art Galleries

A Note on Collecting

AT ONE TIME, all the friends we loved the most were artists. They were the wittiest, the wisest, the poorest, and the most generous. There was no dichotomy between what they wanted and what they did, between weekday life and weekend life. They were the yea-sayers in our microcosm, the distillers of life. Everything we loved in art they taught us.

Stanley William Hayter, Kahlil Gibran II, and Leonard Baskin were our docents. Watching them work, listening to them talk, looking at the world through their eyes were great years in our life. At first we were their affectionate patrons. Owning their works was testament to our symbiosis. Some works were especially meaningful since we had been witness at creation. They were not just ornaments in our house but the maker's presence in our interior landscape.

Our small commitment was rechannelled by the reading, one winter, in the Arizona desert, of Paul Sachs's book, *Modern Prints and Drawings*. It set us on fire. Back east we began to look at and cautiously to buy the prints of our day. We succumbed to Léger, Rouault, Bonnard, Cézanne, Chagall, Miró. We memorialized our first trip to Paris together with two huge Picasso lithographs. And at the closing sale of the Curt Valentin Gallery in 1954 we acquired our first drawings: a Graham Sutherland gouache and a Matisse pen-and-ink.

They exhilarate us still. But that same year, we became friends with Leonard Baskin. What he admired and owned were old master prints and drawings. Until we sat companionably and held them in our hands, we could not believe such affirmations from the past could be seen anywhere outside of a museum. In New York, Walter Schatzki set us loose among his solander boxes. Late that great day we came home with seventeen unattributed old master drawings.

Buying a Picasso or a Matisse is very satisfying. And acquiring an already identified superb old master is surely one of life's joys. But there is nothing more exciting than sitting looking at sheet after sheet, putting aside the ones that have gripped our eye, deciding on the few we cannot live without and bringing them home to discover who is here; what is his country; when is his time; which way has he come?

We started collecting drawings with no other goal than to delight our eye. We have come from an uneducated love and respect for a strong, sure line and the loose, fluid draughtsmanship of the Italian artists, to the complicated world of knowledge that surrounded their making.

We enjoy, now, all the unexpected dividends the drawings have provided: the soothing of our troubled souls, the friendships of art historians and other collectors, dealers, conservators and curators, mat-makers and picture framers. We play endlessly the game of chain-marks and watermarks, collectors' marks and old inscriptions.

Our collection is a modest group, formed in part from the crumbs of the great English collections. But the acquiring of each work is a grand event, from the moment of recognition to our personal commitment. The collection now seems to have a life of its own. We say it *needs* this or it *needs* that, as if it were a precious but demanding ward, temporarily in our custody.

We've found there is no substitute for the experts of this world, for Agnes or Elizabeth Mongan, for Michael Jaffé or Konrad Oberhuber or Ivan Fenyö. We have hitherto unpublished information revealed to us by Agnes Mongan. If you require the undivided attention of a great art historian, learn to be a gourmet cook.

MALCOLM AND ESTHER BICK
Longmeadow, Massachusetts
January, 1971

Introduction

THE RICHNESS and variety of the collection of Italian drawings formed by Dr. and Mrs. Malcolm Bick is clear from the following pages of this catalogue, particularly in the catholicity of the collector's taste, extending over three centuries and the major centers and subjects of Italian art. What is, perhaps, not so readily apparent is the wealth of instruction this collection offers not only in the history of Italian draughtsmanship but into the nature and function of drawings themselves.

Important as drawings are as an independent medium, they often have a relationship with works of art in another medium, and the Bick Collection is remarkable in showing the full range of subtleties of this relationship. While some drawings have no such connection at all, such as a little landscape (no. 9) by an amateur artist known only for his drawings, in others the connection is only marginally closer, as in the work of another amateur, Remigio Cantagallina (nos. 24, 25), who seems to have been an engineer as well as an artist. Cantagallina evidently made these drawings for the sheer pleasure they gave him, but the general subjects—views of towns and mountain roads and streams—did find their way into his etchings. The connection with other media becomes more intimate in a sheet such as the one by Perino del Vaga (no. 4). Here, the artist is putting his first thoughts for a particular fresco down on paper; that the sketches are, in fact, nothing more than thoughts can be seen by their random arrangement across the sheet, on which the artist has even included a list of household expenses. In the same way, Alessandro Magnasco (no. 35) has worked out a group of figures, on the right, which he then used in a painting, although he was probably not thinking in terms of a particular canvas while he was doing the drawing. We are much closer to the finished painting in a study for the *Last Judgment* by Palma Giovane (no. 11), for here we see the artist trying out various poses for a group of figures, including the one that was eventually adopted; he has even added two lines to indicate the corner of the painting for which this sheet is a study. In a drawing that may be from the hand of Taddeo Zuccaro (no. 10), the ideas for a particular fresco in a particular church are being slowly and painstakingly worked out; this drawing is a critical step in the evolution of the design, which was based on another fresco in the same church and was finally executed by the artist's brother. The drawing by Ubaldo Gandolfi (no. 44) is the later of two known preparatory studies for an important ceiling painting and indicates the changes which may occur between what at first sight appears to be the final design and the finished painting. Pellegrino Tibaldi (no. 8) has in fact arrived at the final form of his painting; the differences between this drawing and the completed fresco are negligible. Finally, with the work attributed to Cesare Pollini (no. 14), we feel that there is literally nothing between this and the etching for which it must have been intended; although the etching itself may never have been executed, since no record of it has been found, the careful attention which Pollini gives to every detail of this small but crowded composition, even to the explanatory lettering, indicates that this sheet would have been handed directly to the professional printmaker to copy. Another example of this very close relationship is the drawing by Carlo Maratti (no. 30); here, the master, Maratti, seems to have given his drawing to a member of his studio to complete as a painting, which then formed the basis for a print by still another artist. The Bick Collection also includes drawings (nos. 2, 37) intended directly for stage sets, in one of which the stage flats are numbered; even the height of one of the flats is specified.

The relationship of drawings to works in other media is not confined to preparatory studies and other stages before the fact; they are often records of one kind or another of a completed work. For example, the copy after Sebastiano del Piombo (no. 5) may well have been solely for the man's own recollection of this important fresco; certainly he has not tried to reproduce the whole painting, but only the center and right half of it, and even so, the figure between Christ and his tormentor is just barely indicated in black chalk. Interestingly enough, Sebastiano based his own design for this fresco on a drawing given him by Michelangelo, which survives today only in another drawing after it, by still another artist. The careful study by Fra Antonio Lorenzini (no. 34) is a copy of a painting by a much earlier artist, Andrea del Sarto, which was then used for a print commissioned by the owner of the painting at that time. Finally, we see a drawing (no. 13) not after a work in another medium but after another drawing, which was torn in half, separated into different collections, and finally reunited in the same collection; the Bick copy, aside from its intrinsic charm, is a document of the drawing's original condition.

It should not be forgotten, in the midst of this discussion, that drawings were very often created, and sold, for themselves alone. Even here there is an enormous variety of purposes. The miniature by a late sixteenth-century Venetian artist (no. 17), which could just as easily be considered a finished painting as a drawing, originally formed the frontispiece to a book of laws given by the Doge of Venice to the new mayor of one of the surrounding towns; in other words, the function of the work is as much devotional and, indeed, political, as it is esthetic. Piazzetta's drawings of busts of men and women of different ages, classes, and occupations (no. 38), although sometimes repeated in his paintings, were finished works of art in their own right and must have been sold as such; Ottavio Leoni's prolific activity as a portrait draughtsman (no. 20), surely done on commission and for a fee, was for a slightly different purpose, since he is clearly performing the function of a portrait photographer. Eighteenth-century visitors to Italy also bought caricatures by the hundreds as well as views of the famous sights in Rome and elsewhere; it is difficult to be certain, but the *Sibyl of Cumae* by Pier Leone Ghezzi (no. 36) and the view of the Castel Sant'Angelo (no. 46) may have been intended for this market.

Drawings are also particularly interesting as physical objects, for they often show the effects of having been handed from one artist to another, even from one studio to another. A drawing in the style of Salvator Rosa (no. 33) is like a palimpsest, consisting of several different media and different pieces of paper, executed by two or three artists who added their ideas to the drawing as it passed from hand to hand. Instead of simply adding figures, an artist can also cut them out. The lower left hand corner of the drawing by Domenico Piola (no. 31), with the figures of the Virgin and Child and the donkey, has been cut out and replaced by another sheet with these same figures; stylistic differences between the two sheets may be due to a change in medium or may stem from the possibility that Piola (or another member of his circle) added the second sheet at a later date. The drawing very hesitantly given to Francesco Salviati (no. 6) has been scored on the front and rubbed with red chalk on the back—a sure indication that a copy was made from it.

The paper used by draughtsmen is itself interesting and important—Giovanni Battista Tiepolo's reddish gray paper flecked with red (no. 40) is part of the glory of this beautiful red chalk drawing, the fact that Leoni used blue paper almost exclusively (no. 20) is an important factor in bringing his works together into a coherent body, and the vellum, or animal skin, that Francesco Grigiotti used (no. 21) endows his drawing with a richness of texture ordinary rag paper could not give it. Even more variety is evident in the use of the media themselves, from various colored chalks and inks to washes and even tempera. The different ways in which the same media can be used are illustrated strikingly by two drawings of male heads (nos. 19, 18), both in black and white chalk; the first head is bold and powerful, filling the page, while the second retreats within the paper, hesitant and delicate.

The individual entries of this catalogue have, on the whole, attempted to place each drawing within its art historical context; it is, of course, not possible within the compass of a short introduction to provide an adequate history of Italian draughtsmanship. Nevertheless, the reader of the catalogue, and the visitor to the exhibition, may find it profitable to compare drawings produced in the same city but in different centuries; for example, the exuberance of Palma Giovane's *Last Judgment* (no. 11) is not far from that of Gian Battista Crosato (no. 41), both of which were drawn in Venice, but separated in time by almost 150 years. Differences of approach to a particular subject are also notable: the careful, almost tight control of a landscape by Domenico Campagnola (no. 3) gives way to the freshness and informality of a Cantagallina (no. 25). Perhaps most interesting is to see how these drawings embody several of the main trends of Italian art from the early sixteenth to the late eighteenth century. The tight grouping of figures in the Zuccaro (no. 10), with its sharp contrasts of light and shadow, changes in direction, and energetic poses, is certainly far distant from the rococo openness of Crosato (no. 41), Gandolfi (no. 44), and Gaspare Diziani (no. 39), where light and empty space—empty paper—fill the areas between the clusters of gesturing figures. The classical baroque is also well represented in the Bick Collection, with examples illustrating the desire to reinstate the masterpieces of High Renaissance painting (no. 34) and the goals of compositional clarity and stability (nos. 23, 30). In fact, just within the context of a single artist's work, drawings can become sensitive reflections of shifts of taste. A drawing given to Guercino (no. 22) and extremely typical of his earlier period shows the realism, spontaneity, sharp contrasts of light and shadow, of early seventeenth-century Caravaggism, whereas a later drawing of high quality from the artist's hand (no. 23) has a more careful, finished character typical of much of the classical baroque. A late eighteenth-century imitation of Guercino's early style by Pietro Giacomo Palmieri (no. 45), transforms the earlier master's directness and energy into a rococo decorativeness typical of contemporary productions in France, where, in fact, this drawing was done.

Inevitably, there are some drawings which cannot be identified precisely in terms of time, place, and authorship; a striking example of this is a powerful drawing of a man's head (no. 19), about which we have been able to say very little. It is hoped that its publication here will eventually lead to its proper identification. However, such a work reminds us of the ultimate purpose of a catalogue such as this: the work of art itself, finally, must stand alone, independent of its function, its condition, its relationship to other works of art or its historical importance. Any exhibition achieves its vitality not only from drawings of such high quality, which are common in this collection, but also true masterpieces, such as the Piazzetta (no. 38), which are uncommon in any collection.

The editors of this catalogue and the students who worked on the various entries would like to thank the collectors, Dr. and Mrs. Bick, for their generosity and patience throughout this whole project; they have been particularly kind in entrusting the heart of their very large collection of drawings to our study, and to whatever conclusions, correct or incorrect, that we would come to. It is unusual, to say the least, for the owners of such beautiful drawings to permit them to be off their walls for the duration of a seminar and an extended exhibition schedule, a period of almost two years. The editors would also like to thank the students who worked so hard on this catalogue; their response to an unusually demanding seminar has been stimulating to us as teachers.

F.W.R.

J.T.P.

The Catalogue

The catalogue entries were compiled by the following students:

URY BALDUN

THOMAS M. DEMARCO

JANICE G. FULLMAN

KAREN L. GOODMAN

SUSAN K. HAMILTON

NANCY M. HANDELMAN

ANN S. HURD

KEVIN KANE

ROBERT H. LAVENDA

GREGORY K. SCHELKUN

PETER C. SORLIEN

BRADFORD WATTERS

JAMES A. WERKOWSKI

In the dimensions of each drawing, height precedes width. "Lugt" in the catalogue refers to Frits Lugt, *Les Marques de Collections*, The Hague, 1956 (1921), with Supplement. A number of the drawings included in this exhibition were also shown at the John and Mable Ringling Museum of Art, Sarasota, in December, 1970.

ANDREA DEL SARTO
Florence, 1486 – Florence, 1530

1 HEAD OF A BOY

Red chalk; laid down. Water stain lower right. 132 by 144 mm.; 5 3/16 by 5 1/2 in.

Inscribed by a later hand, in pen and brown ink, *Andrea del Sarto*.

PROVENANCE: A. Caselli (1968).

Sidney J. Freedberg has confirmed the attribution of this drawing, placing it in the decade of the 1520s, the last of Andrea's life. This drawing is most probably from Andrea's transitional moment of 1527, after his classicizing period, but before his experimentation with mannerism. The modeling and play of light on the face, typical of his studies of youthful faces (Freedberg, pls. 70, 107, 140), mark Andrea's studies in this, his favorite medium. However, these earlier sketches are far more vigorous, more fully articulated, and more heavily shadowed, with heavier, stronger strokes of the chalk. The chalk of our drawing has been rubbed, adding to the less assertive quality of the work. Despite the carefully worked features, this drawing seems spontaneous. The tilt of the head, the forcing of the figure off the page, the tousled hair, and the incompleteness give a freer look than the picture actually warrants. This drawing may be a study for putti in the painting of *The Sacrifice of Isaac* in Dresden or Madrid (Freedberg, pls. 190, 191) or the *Assumption of the Virgin* in the Pitti (Freedberg, pl. 196). However, in both cases the turning of the heads is slightly more pronounced than in our drawing and a precise counterpart to the Bick drawing cannot be found in Andrea's paintings.

BIBLIOGRAPHY: Sidney J. Freedberg, *Andrea del Sarto*, Cambridge, 1963; John K. G. Shearman, *Andrea del Sarto*, Oxford, 1965.

N.M.H.

Attributed to GIULIO ROMANO
Rome, 1499 – Mantua, 1546

2 A PORCH OF THE MAIDENS

Black chalk; laid down. Left edge, 234 mm., 9 1/4 in.; right edge, 303 mm., 12 in.; width, 227 mm., 9 15/16 in.

Center, in black chalk, *1535*; lower right in pen and brown ink, in a later hand, *B. v Cellino*. Marks of the Lanier Collection, Lugt 2885, Cosway Collection, Lugt 628, Abbott Collection (twice), Lugt 970, Chariatte Collection, Lugt 88a. Verso, marks of the Chariatte Collection and Reitlinger Collection, Lugt 2274a.

PROVENANCE: N. Lanier; R. Cosway; F. Abbott; A. Chariatte; H. S. Reitlinger; A. Caselli (1968).

andrea del sarto

1

Michael Jaffé was the first to attribute this drawing to Giulio Romano and has (by letter) compared it to pen and ink *modelli* for frescoes at the Palazzo del Té (Hartt, figs. 164, 165). In addition there is a similar handling of heads and draperies in a study of an *Allegory of the Virtues of Federigo Gonzaga* (ca. 1529–34, British Museum, no. 79), also from the Lanier collection, and in drawings of Dawn (ca. 1534–40, B.M. no. 80) and of *A Woman Standing on a Dragon* (ca. 1540–46, B.M. no. 82), the latter also from the Cosway collection.

As an assistant to Raphael, Giulio would have seen caryatids used as decorative motifs as early as 1512–14 in the Stanza d'Eliodoro at the Vatican (Salmi, p. 204, fig. 11). Later, Giulio did studies for herm-caryatids for the Stanza dell'Incendio and assisted in rendering telamon figures there as well (Salmi, pp. 219–220, figs. 40–44). Caryatids appear again in the Sala di Costantino (Hartt, figs. 57, 59). Giulio's fresco of a nymphaeum which decorates a window embrasure there includes a portico supported by two sets of three-faced caryatids adorned in the same braided hair and draperies as those of the present drawing (Hartt, fig. 75). The same hair and clothing styles are present on caryatids in an engraving of a monumental façade by Marcantonio Raimondi, another collaborator of Raphael (Salmi, p. 511 ff., fig. 33). Also, caryatids are illustrated in various contemporary books, for example, in the 1511 Venice and 1521 Como editions of Vitruvius.

This drawing may be a study for temporary stage or pageant architecture. Giulio was exposed to the new interest in stage design during his apprenticeship in Raphael's workshop (Badt, p. 43 ff.), and throughout his residence in Mantua designed many plays, pageants, and festivals for the Gonzaga court (Hartt, p. 72). Mantua's important theatrical tradition dates from at least 1471, and only three years after Giulio's death a permanent theatre was erected there (Kennard, pp. 158–160, 164–166). Caryatids, admittedly unusual in this context at this time, would seem to satisfy a Vitruvian suggestion that classical statuary be included in tragic scenes (cf. Krautheimer, pp. 327–346), and herm-caryatids did appear in Buontalenti's set for the *intermezzo* of 1589 (Nagler, fig. 51). Sixteenth-century stage design relied upon pronounced orthogonals to create the illusion of perspective depth, a function provided by the heavy cornice and rectilinear bases of the caryatids in the Bick drawing. The left edge of the drawing is clearly delineated by a vertical line, indicating that the drawing was not cut from a larger composition, as one might at first suppose.

The first known owner of this drawing was Nicholas Lanier, who in 1628 was one of the intermediaries in the purchase of the collection of the Dukes of Mantua. Lanier also sometimes kept numbers of drawings for himself (Lugt, 1, p. 533), and the Bick drawing may have come to him directly from that collection.

BIBLIOGRAPHY: Kurt Badt, "Raphael's 'Incendio del Borgo'," *Journal of the Warburg and Courtauld Institutes*, XXII, 1959; J. A. Gere and Philip Pouncey, *Italian Drawings in the Department of Prints and Drawings in the British Museum: Raphael and His Circle*, London, 1962; Frederick Hartt, *Giulio Romano*, New Haven, 1958; Joseph Spencer Kennard, *The Italian Theatre*, I, New York, 1932; Richard Krautheimer, "The Tragic and Comic Scenes of the Renaissance," *Gazette des Beaux-Arts*, XXXIII, 1948; Frits Lugt, *Marques des Collections*, The Hague, 1956 (1921); A. M. Nagler, *Theatre Festivals of the Medici 1539–1637*, New Haven, 1964; Mario Salmi, ed., *The Complete Works of Raphael*, New York, 1969.

J.A.W.

2

DOMENICO CAMPAGNOLA

Padua, 1500 – Padua, 1581

3 HILLY LANDSCAPE WITH WOMAN AND DONKEY

Pen and brown ink. Watermark: six-pointed star on top of crown. 245 by 381 mm.; 9⅝ by 13 1/16 in.

Verso, in pen and brown ink, *motfias*.

PROVENANCE: A. Caselli (1968).

This superb drawing is very similar to a number of other works attributed to the Venetian master Domenico Campagnola. In particular, a drawing in the art market in New York (Shickman, 1968, no. 11) is close in its handling of the surface of the ground, of the trees, and of the "sculpted" rocks, but is most striking in that it, too, has overdrawing in the right foreground. The original short lines, defining details of the terrain, have been covered by long flowing ones, smoothing out and simplifying the surface of the ground. This work is also similar to drawings in Bayonne (no. 16) and in the Kunsthalle, Hamburg (no. 18). Common to the Bick and Hamburg drawings in particular are clusters of short, wiry lines that define, for example, one face of a rock, set next to another cluster that moves in an opposite direction, creating a restless surface of the ground. Another characteristic common to these two drawings is a tendency to define the edge of a mound or some other low swelling on the ground by one or two long strokes, against which the clusters of short strokes within the area are juxtaposed; the end result is to give the feeling of a profile and even the sense of a series of stage flats. Whether these are characteristics typical of Campagnola himself or of one of his most gifted followers is difficult to determine; nonetheless, many of the best drawings attributed to Campagnola manifest them.

Campagnola's work popularized the graphic style of Venetian landscape created by Titian and Giorgione, and was often copied even into the eighteenth century. Watteau, for example, made copies of drawings either by Campagnola himself, or in his style.

BIBLIOGRAPHY: Keith Andrews, *National Gallery of Scotland, Catalogue of Italian Drawings*, Cambridge, 1968; Otto Benesch, *Disegni veneti dell'Albertina di Vienna*, Venice, 1961; Jacob Bean, *Inventaire Générale des Dessins des Musées de Province Bayonne: Dessins de la Collection Bonnat*, Paris, 1960; *Exhibition of Old Master Drawings at the H. Shickman Gallery*, New York, 1968; Agnes Mongan and Paul J. Sachs, *Drawings in the Fogg Museum of Art*, Cambridge, Mass., 1940; Larissa Salmina, *Disegni veneti del Museo di Leningrado*, Venice, 1964; Felice Stampfle and Jacob Bean, *Drawings from New York Collections I*, New York, 1965; Wolf Stubbe, *Hundert Meisterzeichnungen aus der Hamburger Kunsthalle*, Hamburg, 1967.

R.H.L.

PERINO DEL VAGA

Florence, 1501 – Rome, 1547

4 TWENTY-THREE FIGURES IN VARIOUS SCENES AND POSES

VERSO: in the artist's hand, five figures in scenes of battle and a list of expenses.

Pen and brown ink. Horizontal center fold. 192 by 274 mm.; 7⅝ by 10¹³⁄₁₆ in.

Inscribed, in pen and brown ink, *P. del Vaga*; upper left on a repaired corner, in pen and brown ink, *741*; marks of the Mayor collection, Lugt 2799, the Lely collection, Lugt 2092, and the Richardson collection, Lugt 2183. Verso, in pen and brown ink, *Perino 69*; also on the verso in pen and ink, in two different hands (?), a list of expenses, such as a table, a bedspread, a table cloth, napkins, and biscuits (see below).

PROVENANCE: Peter Lely; Jonathan Richardson, senior; W. Mayor; W. Schatzki (1955).

Perino del Vaga, also known as Pietro Buonaccorsi, was born in Florence in 1501 and entered the workshop of Ridolfo Ghirlandaio by the age of eleven. During this very early period he drew mostly from Michelangelo's cartoons of the *Battle of Cascina* and in 1515 he left for Rome with another artist called Vaga, from whom he acquired his pseudonym. Except for a short sojourn in Florence around 1523, he remained in Rome until 1528 in the workshop of Raphael. Here he joined the master's pupils in the decoration of the Vatican Loggie.

Primarily a draughtsman and designer rather than a fresco painter, Perino left Rome in 1528 in order to avoid the widespread work shortage and the devastating effects of the sack of the city in 1527. The artist in the same year arrived in Genoa and sought employment under Prince Andrea Doria, who was admiral of the Pope's fleet; he was also in the process of completing a sizable palace on the Ligurian coast. This was to be Perino's first significant independent commission and it was here that his style matured during the years 1528–33.

Two years after his arrival in Genoa Perino was working in the Sala dei Trionfi, a ground floor vestibule in the Palazzo Doria. This great room was decorated with four triumphant scenes of which two have been definitely identified: the *Triumph of Bacchus in India* and the *Triumph of the Roman Consul Aemilius Paulus*. Within the spandrels surrounding the ceiling decoration Perino painted the Olympian gods and goddesses, largely drawn from his experience with the school of Raphael.

The figure study at hand was probably done by Perino as one of his many preliminary studies for the Sala dei Trionfi. Among the twenty-three figures on the recto some apply to the gods while the rest are suited to military scenes. For example, the central figure on the top of the sheet wears a helmet-type headdress with wings and has been drawn in the classical pose of Mercury. Another figure in the upper left of the sheet appears almost to be a Roman centurion, which Perino could have drawn from an ancient sarcophagus. The remaining figures almost all seem to be portrayed in violent or martial poses. Both of these themes again point to this drawing being connected with the Sala dei Trionfi.

Stylistically one can find a close counterpart to this sheet in another study of figures in the Uffizi (Davidson, 1966, no. 30, figs. 28 and 29). Bernice Davidson has ascribed the latter drawing to Perino's Genoese period and has also confirmed orally that the Bick drawing falls into this category. Miss Davidson has pointed out that in Genoa Michelangelo's influence on Perino gradually faded and he eventually developed a style that was almost purely decorative, emptied of all emotional content or even dramatic expression. The figures on this sheet obviously still possess a significant degree of emotional content, again pointing to Perino's first few years of work in Genoa, more specifically the Sala dei Trionfi.

Unfortunately, much of the decoration in the Palazzo Doria has been destroyed and it is therefore impossible to make any specific correlation between the figures in this drawing and those in the ceiling decorations. The very preliminary nature of this drawing also prohibits precise comparison with the ceiling figures. Nevertheless, both the content and style suggest Perino's early period in Genoa and particularly the frescoes at the Sala dei Trionfi with their scenes of Olympian gods and military triumphs.

BIBLIOGRAPHY: Bernice Davidson, *Perino del Vaga e la sua Cerchia*, Uffizi, Florence, 1966; Bernice Davidson, "Drawings by Perino del Vaga for the Palazzo Doria," *Art Bulletin*, 1959; Pamela Askew, "Perino del Vaga's Decorations for the Palazzo Doria, Genoa," *Burlington Magazine*, 1956, p. 46; J. A. Gere, "Two Late Fresco Cycles by Perino del Vaga," *Burlington Magazine*, 1960.

T.M.D.

The inscription on the verso reads as follows:

quarro lenzola costorno – ——	
Elcortinagio costo – — —	
u[n] pano celonelu[n]go	guli — 8
unaltro largo —	guli — 8
unatavola lu[n]ga	guli — 4
la larga co[n] suo sopra ba[n]cho	guli 4
u[n] forziera —	guli 7
i[n] . . . . [?] tovaglia grosa lu[n]ga	guli 7
unaltra pezo sotile .3. rova. . [?]	guli 3
dua iscusie dan[n]otte di tabi	gli 7
una iscoperta ispediio [?] una chalza /tora —	gli 3
alchavallo coletto	glili 8
u[n] chapezala di piuma	guli — 9
i[n] portature —	guli — 1
Una coperta da letto	guli — 1.9 [?]
i[n] pennelli —	glili — 3
per du sedie du ba[n]di[n]ttiglli	— 4
mi[n] [?] par di chalze alpuro	guli — 10
per dua corrolli [?] dua tempera	guli — 4
pen[n]e —	guli —
per u[n] corrello gra[n]de u[n] cano[n] di stagna [?]	gli — 13
per u[n] sacone Cioe latela pagli	guli — 6
per bodiolj fiasci gotti du marinaroi [?] —	guli 23 [?]
per du fiasci coperti di notrie [?] —	gli — 1
per portatura duna . . asata di biscotte gli	10
i[n] nu[n] par difasani	gli — 8
i[n] nu[n] marzapane una scatola dicopeta	
una feguza dinodriata —	gli — [?]

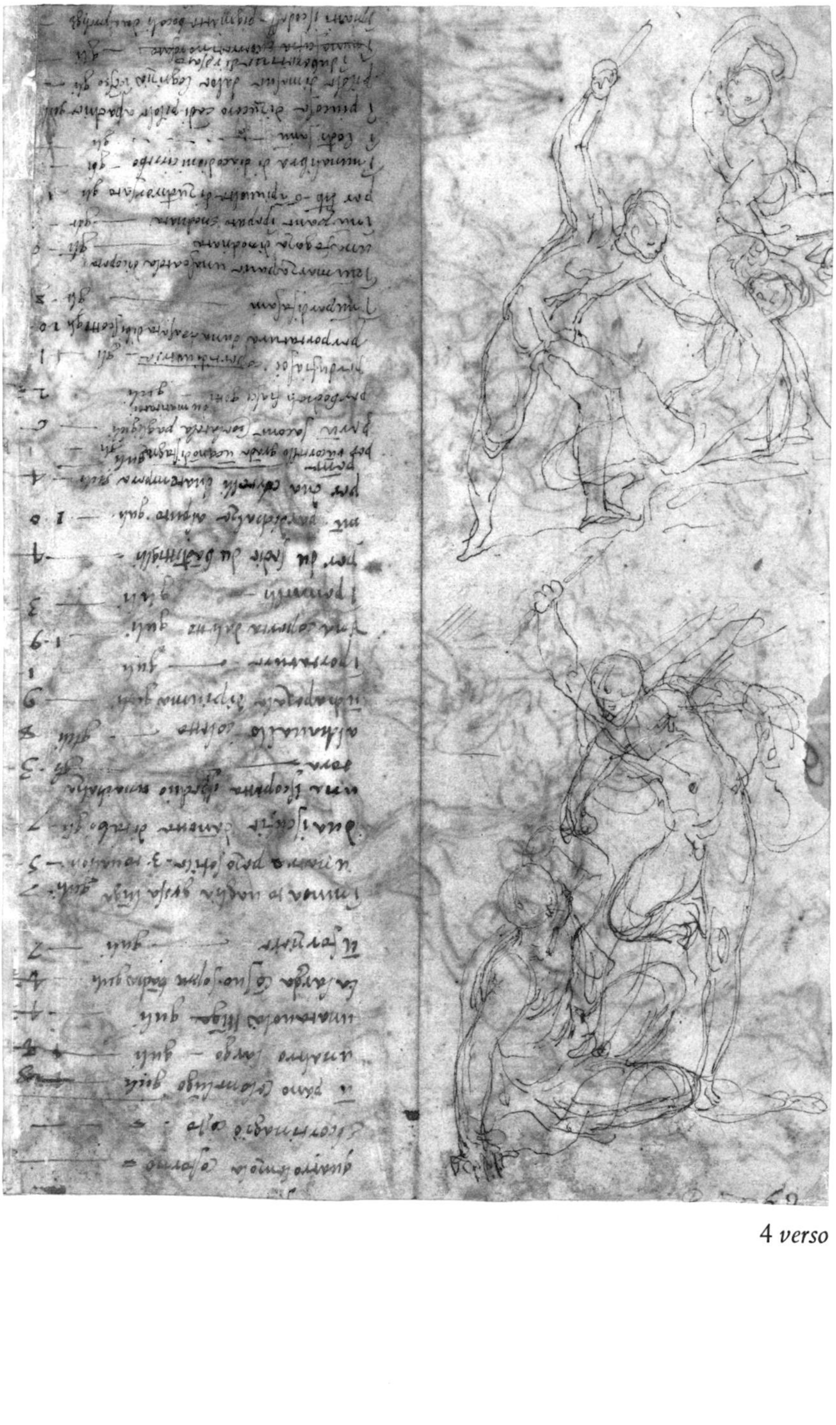

4 *verso*

i[n] nu[n] pane i[n] pepato snodriata — gli — [?]
per lib[bre] 6 i[n] piu volte di zuxtinorsato [?] gli 1
i[n] nuna libra di diacodioni cirrebo — gli
i[n] lodi [?] sanu — gli —
i[n] piu cose dizucero ce[n] di pilole apadie [?] gli
pilole di mesue dalor logrizia i[n] ce[n]sso [?] gli —
i[n] du pererine dirosato — gli —
i[n] nuna scifia e uberretino rosato [*crossed out*]
i[n] piatto iscodel . . . pigniatte bocali dualperch [?] gli —

[More of the inscription is hidden by the mat at the top and the bottom.]

After SEBASTIANO DEL PIOMBO

Venice, ca. 1485 – Rome, 1547

5 FLAGELLATION OF CHRIST

Pen and brown ink, brown wash, heightened with white, black chalk. 420 by 327 mm.; 16¾ by 12¾ in.

Verso, in pen and brown ink, *Primaticcio il Quadro a Fontanablu; 43.*

PROVENANCE: Skippe (lot 326, November 20/21, 1958); A. Caselli (1968).

Sebastiano del Piombo, originally a Venetian, was a popular and successful painter practicing in Rome in the first quarter of the sixteenth century. There he was befriended by Michelangelo, who, in addition to helping Sebastiano gain commissions, also provided designs for some of his works and otherwise greatly influenced his style. This association made Sebastiano the rival of Raphael and an influential figure in the art world of Rome.

Sebastiano's fresco of the *Flagellation* was completed in the years 1516–24 for the Borgherini Chapel in San Pietro in Montorio, a church complex which contains great monuments by Bernini, Baburen, and Bramante. The Bick drawing is most likely a copy of this *Flagellation*. The central figure between Christ and the grimacing man at the right (barely visible in the photographic reproduction) is all but eliminated from the drawing, which would not be the case if this were a cartoon. Moreover, the identical detailing of the drawing and the fresco in nearly all particulars suggests that the larger version—the fresco—was the model. Finally, other examples of Sebastiano's cartoons are unlike the Bick drawing (Shearman, pl. 24d). This drawing, then, is one of many copies of the *Flagellation* which indicate how important the painting was in its own time, more as a reflection of Michelangelo's art than of Sebastiano's. Giulio Clovio, in fact, seems to have made a copy directly from Michelangelo's drawing rather than from Sebastiano's fresco (Popham and Wilde, no. 451, fig. 100), thus further emphasizing the primacy of Michelangelo's role in this venture.

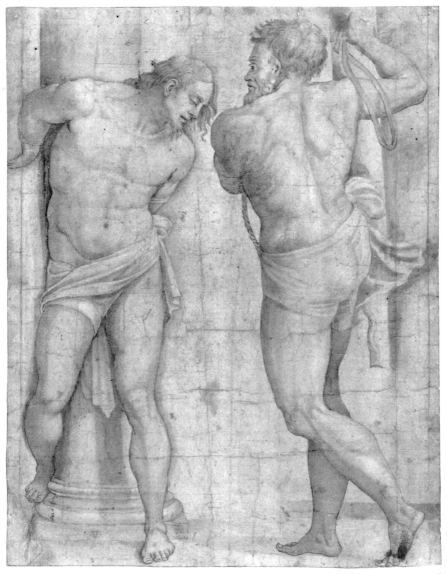

5

BIBLIOGRAPHY: Bernard Berenson, *The Drawings of the Florentine Painters*, I, Chicago, 1938; Oskar Fischel, "A New Approach to Sebastiano del Piombo as a Draughtsman," *Old Master Drawings*, XIV, June, 1939; Sydney J. Freedberg, *Painting of the High Renaissance in Rome and Florence*, Cambridge, 1961: Michael Hirst, "The Chigi Chapel in S. Maria della Pace," *Journal of the Warburg and Courtauld Institutes*, XXIV, 1961; A. E. Popham and Johannes Wilde, *The Italian Drawings of the XV and XVI Centuries in the Collection of His Majesty the King at Windsor Castle*, London, 1949; John Shearman, "The Chigi Chapel in S. Maria della Pace," *Journal of the Warburg and Courtauld Institutes*, XXIV, 1961; Johannes Wilde, *Italian Drawings in the Department of Prints and Drawings in the British Museum, Michelangelo and His Studio*, London, 1953.

B.W.

Attributed to FRANCESCO SALVIATI

Florence, 1510 – Florence, 1563

6 TWO WARRIORS SUPPORTING ESCUTCHEONS

Pen and brown ink. The drawing has been scored, and the verso has been rubbed with red chalk. 271 by 201 mm.; $10\frac{11}{16}$ by $8\frac{3}{16}$ in.

Mark of the Reynolds Collection, Lugt 2364. Verso, in pen and ink, *1665*: in pen and ink, *Perino di grande intelli/genza e pratica* (indecipherable figures) /*J. R. Ang.* (or *Aug.*), Lugt 2983–2984.

PROVENANCE: Jonathan Richardson; Sir Joshua Reynolds; A. Wolmark; A. Mathews (1959).

This drawing corresponds exactly to a drawing attributed to Giorgio Vasari (Ashmolean, no. 740), even including the third figure in the lower right; the two drawings were in the same collections in the eighteenth century. The Ashmolean drawing and a second sketch given to Vasari, in the Art Institute, Chicago (*Age of Vasari*, D43), are closely related to tondos of the districts of Florence for the ceiling of the Sala Grande of the Palazzo Vecchio in Florence (*Age of Vasari*, D43a). The Bick drawing and its Ashmolean counterpart deal with the lower section of these tondos. The Ashmolean catalogue mentions the Bick drawing (p. 396), calling it "a contemporary copy." This raises the problem of whether the Bick drawing is the original or the copy. The Bick drawing has red chalk on the back and scoring on the front, a typical method used for tracing a drawing. Christopher Lloyd has been kind enough to inform us (by letter) that the Ashmolean drawing has no such marks.

It is difficult to know to whom the Bick drawing should be attributed. Francesco Salviati has been suggested; although Salviati's late drawings (the Vasari tondos are from the last year of Salviati's life) are usually in pen and ink with wash, the sketchiness and stylization of the drawings, the curling, cloud-like manner of representing the human figure less as an anatomical figure and more as an ornamental device, accord well with this drawing. In addition, Salviati, who was in Florence in 1563, was a friend of Vasari and the two artists often worked together and had copied each other's work. Mrs. Iris Cheney has pointed out that at this

6

time they were in contact since antagonisms had arisen between Salviati and Daniele da Volterra and Pirro Ligorio in Rome, and Vasari had been trying to help him out of his difficulties. Final determination of the relationship of the two drawings to each other, to Vasari's paintings, and to other sixteenth-century masters must await further research.

BIBLIOGRAPHY: Bryan, *Dictionary of Painters and Engravers*, II, London, 1904; Iris Cheney, *Francesco Salviati*, Ann Arbor, 1963; K. T. Parker, *Catalogue of the Collection of Drawings in the Ashmolean Museum*, Oxford, 1965; Irving I. Zupnick, *The Age of Vasari*, Binghamton, 1970.

N.M.H.

LUCA CAMBIASO
Moneglia, 1527 – Escorial, 1585

7 HOLY FAMILY WITH ST. JOHN

Pen and brown ink, light brown wash on tan paper. 225 by 345 mm.; 8 ¾ by 13 ½ in.

Old inscription in black chalk, lower right, *Luca Ca. . . genova*; inventory number, in pen and black ink, *152*.

PROVENANCE: W. Schatzki (1955).

Luca Cambiaso, "Il Luchetto," was first taught by his father, Giovanni, a fresco painter of lesser merit. Perino del Vaga, Correggio, Titian, and most importantly, Galeazzo Alessi influenced the young Luca.

The finest works of Cambiaso come during the years between 1550 and 1580. His major pieces fall into three phases of development: first, a gigantic manner of panel decoration in collaboration with his father; second, an intermediate Raphaelesque, Roman style, less mannered than Perino's, which in the 1550s evolved into a style influenced by Venetian trends; and finally in the 1570s, a serene style characterized by subdued pastels and simplified forms.

The attribution of drawings to Cambiaso presents a great problem to the art historian. Even during his lifetime, his drawings were widely sought after, and often copied and used for studies. Another problem is that the Holy Family was one of Cambiaso's favorite themes, repeated many times throughout his life in ever varying interpretations. Although the Bick drawing is related to a painting by Cambiaso of the same subject (Frabetti, pl. 20) in Genoa, ca. 1560, many more of the artist's drawings and copies after his drawings are known than his paintings. Many of Cambiaso's drawings can be found in American collections, but most of his paintings remain in Genoa. The present work is particularly similar in style and format to an unpublished drawing attributed to Cambiaso of the *Holy Family* from the Egmont Album at Yale; Mrs. Mary Newcome has pointed out (by letter) the dramatic similarity of this drawing with one of the same subject in the Rosenwald collection, Jenkintown.

BIBLIOGRAPHY: G. Frabetti and A. M. Gabrielli, *Luca Cambiaso e la sua Fortuna*, Genoa, 1956; Robert L. Manning, *Drawings of Luca Cambiaso*, New York, 1967; Robert and Bertina Suida Manning, *Genoese Masters*, 1963.

G.K.S.

PELLEGRINO TIBALDI

Bologna, 1527 – Milan, 1596

8 STUDY FOR A PRESENTATION OF THE VIRGIN AT THE TEMPLE

Pen and brown ink and grey wash; the column on the right has been finished in red chalk by a later hand. Vertical center fold; the drawing has been arched and laid down. 395 by 240 mm.; 15 $\frac{7}{16}$ by 9 $\frac{7}{16}$ in.

PROVENANCE: A. Caselli (1968).

Pellegrino Tibaldi was a Bolognese mannerist painter and architect. While a student in Rome in 1547, he intensively studied the works of Michelangelo, who remained the dominant influence on Tibaldi's style throughout his entire career. He then returned to Bologna and for many years afterwards was active as a fresco painter there, and also as a successful architect in Milan. In 1586 Philip II called Tibaldi to the Spanish court to succeed Federico Zuccaro in decorating the library and cloisters of the Escorial. For the ceiling of the library Tibaldi was responsible for depicting a highly involved religious-philosophical scheme of decoration. In the lower cloisters Tibaldi erased Zuccaro's work to present scenes from the life of the Virgin and Christ. As Briganti has pointed out (*Manierismo e Pellegrino Tibaldi*, p. 90), one of his major considerations was balancing the formal masses of the painting with the heavy architecture of the Escorial. After completion of the commission in 1592, Tibaldi returned to Milan where he was appointed architect for the Duomo, a post he held until his death.

Miles L. Chappell has been responsible for the correct attribution for this drawing. It is clearly a preliminary sketch for a large arched fresco of the Presentation of the Virgin, one of five frescoes of the life of Mary that Tibaldi executed in the lower cloisters. Tibaldi made some changes from the sketch in the fresco itself; the poses of the beggars are altered; the bird cage in the lower right is missing; two steps have been added in front of the columns. The blank area in the lower right-hand corner contains five figures in the fresco: Mary, her parents, and two onlookers. The directional gaze of the first beggar and the high priest is indicative of the omitted figures; however, the problem may have proved too complex for Tibaldi to handle on this small a scale. The sketch is a finer work than the fresco, which today is overblown and lifeless. Tibaldi may have used assistants for the actual painting of the fresco, or the effects of temperature and moisture, against which the cloister is not well protected, may have severely damaged the works. Venturi (p. 573) speaks of repainting of the frescoes in modern times and there may have been earlier retouchings. Another preparatory study for a painting by Tibaldi in the Escorial is reproduced in *Les Dessins Italiens de la Reine Christine de Suède* (pl. 43), and in the British Museum (no. 115) there is a design for the decoration of the library of the Escorial, also in pen and brown ink and wash, but in a larger size.

8

BIBLIOGRAPHY: Giuliano Briganti, *Italian Mannerism*, Leipzig, 1962; Giuliano Briganti, *Manierismo e Pellegrino Tibaldi*, Rome, 1945; Julien Zarco Cuevas, *Pintores Italianos en San Lorenzo el Real de el Escorial (1575–1613)*, Madrid, 1932; *Italian Drawings of the XVI Century*, British Museum, 1951; J. Q. van Regteren Altena, *Les Dessins Italiens de la Reine Christine de Suède*, Stockholm, 1966; A. Venturi, *Storia Dell'Arte Italiana*, ix, 6, Milan, 1933. For the most recent review of the literature on Tibaldi drawings, see *Le XVI. Siècle Européen*, Petit Palais, Paris, 1965, pp. 225, 227.

N.M.H.

MESSER ULISSE SEVERINO DA CINGOLI

1536/1542 – 1597/1600

9 HOUSE IN A LANDSCAPE

Pen and brown ink, brown and white wash, on blue paper. 145 by 212 mm.; 5 ¾ by 8 ⅜ in.

Upper left, traces of an inscription, in pen and ink; verso, in pencil, *9*.

PROVENANCE: N. Chaikin.

A recent attribution of this and approximately 150 other drawings in the same hand to Messer Ulisse Severino da Cingoli has been made by J. Bolten. Previously attributed mainly to Flemish artists such as Bartholomeus Spranger and Matthijs Cock, or to an occasional Italian artist such as Polidoro da Caravaggio, the drawings have been given to Messer Ulisse because of the likeness between his signature on the cover of an album of landscape drawings in the Biblioteca Comunale in Jesi, and the handwriting of the inscriptions on some of the drawings themselves.

According to Bolten, Messer Ulisse belonged to a distinguished family and was well educated, as is indicated by the fashionable Italian written in the inscriptions on his work. Several factors reveal his probable lack of professional artistic training, including his often improper use of perspective. Lists of household medicines, prices of cereals and wines, and notes on properties and owners on the verso of some of his drawings indicate Messer Ulisse's interests to have been those of a country squire. His drawings are most likely visual mementos of an artist's rambles outdoors, created solely for their own sake.

The drawing shows an unidentifiable structure of curious architectural style, set in a grove of trees. Two types are distinguishable among the landscape drawings of Messer Ulisse: romantic views inspired by an actual site or borrowed from works of other artists, and topographically correct representations of rivers, hills, or grounds often identified in inscriptions as being located in the Marches. Included in the latter category are quick studies of sites and sketches of rocks, trees, houses, and hamlets, and it is in this group that the Bick drawing seems to belong. This is perhaps one of his earlier works as its style resembles his drawings of the 1560s (e.g. Bolten, pl. 4, no. 135) and is less free and detailed than in many of his later works (Bolten, pl. 7, no. 152).

No instances are known, according to Bolten, of borrowing from Messer Ulisse, probably because his social position, the place where he lived, and the

nature of his artistic activity set him apart from the artistic centers of his day. The direct sources of influence on his own style are not known, though he probably did borrow from the Flemish landscape tradition. No other works of art besides landscape drawings are attributed to Messer Ulisse, and he is the only known sixteenth-century Italian artist who produced solely this type of work.

BIBLIOGRAPHY: J. Bolten, "Messer Ulisse Severino da Cingoli, a Bypath in the History of Art," *Master Drawings*, VII, 2, 1969; Heinrich Gerhard Franz, *Niederländische Landschaftsmalerei im Zeitalter des Manierismus*, Graz, 1969.

K.L.G.

Attributed to TADDEO ZUCCARO
Sant'Angelo del Vado, 1529 – Rome, 1566

10 THE ASSUMPTION OF THE VIRGIN

Pen and brown ink, brown wash, squared for transfer in the lower half in red chalk (by a later hand?) and by a third hand, in the upper half, in pencil. Arched, 250 by 145 mm.; 10 by 5 7/8 in.

In pencil by a later hand, *Domenichino*; mark of the West collection, Lugt 419.

PROVENANCE: Benjamin West; A. Caselli (1968).

This sixteenth-century mannerist drawing was instrumental in the evolution of a fresco of the *Assumption of the Virgin* in Santa Trinità dei Monti in Rome. Taddeo Zuccaro was originally commissioned to do the work by Pope Pius IV in 1563; however, the project was still unfinished three years later at the artist's death in 1566 and his younger brother Federico was given the commission, which he completed in 1589. J. A. Gere's detailed study of the preliminary drawings by both artists for the fresco has clarified the subtle differences between the approaches to the problem by the two brothers.

There seems to be little doubt that the Bick drawing is closely related to the various drawings by the Zuccari for this fresco. The basic source for Taddeo's drawings for this fresco was another fresco in the same church also of the *Assumption of the Virgin* by Daniele da Volterra, which is characterized by a remarkable detail of the ascent of the Virgin through a circular opening in the roof of a round, colonnaded building. In the Bick drawing the Virgin is ascending up into what seems to be a dome-like structure with a circular opening at the top, echoed by a semicircular ring of angels surrounding her. In the completed fresco by Federico this distinctive feature, the opening, has disappeared. The Bick drawing is a transitional step between Daniele's and Federico's versions also in placement of the tomb. In Taddeo's drawing (Gere, 1966, fig. 10) it is diagonal to the picture frame, while in this drawing and in the completed fresco it is perpendicular to it. The arching of the composition is found again in a drawing, now in the Uffizi, after Taddeo by Federico (Gere, 1966, fig. 12); the fresco was painted in a rectangular space. Most importantly, as Gere points out (1966, p. 288), Taddeo had solved the

Domenichino

10

problem of relating the upper and lower halves of the composition by creating a ring of apostles below and a ring of angels above, with a circle or opening above the Virgin herself—essentially the composition of the Bick drawing. Such an organization is totally absent in the completed fresco, an indication of how much the final solution was the work of Federico, influenced though he may have been by Taddeo's ideas.

Stylistically, this drawing is close to preparatory sketches for this fresco; for example, in a study of an apostle standing by the sarcophagus attributed by Gere to Taddeo (1966, fig. 7), the two extended arms on opposite sides of the tomb are strikingly similar to those in the drawing at hand. In the completed fresco the Virgin's arms are extended while in the drawing after Taddeo by Federico (Gere, 1966, fig. 12) the Virgin's hands are clasped over her heart, a pose also present in the Bick drawing.

Taddeo labored again and again at a suitable solution for the final fresco and through his last drawings one can follow the process through which his conception developed. The Bick drawing may well have been one step in this evolution.

BIBLIOGRAPHY: J. A. Gere, "Two of Taddeo Zuccaro's Commissions Completed by Federico Zuccaro in the Pucci Chapel in Santa Trinità dei Monti, I, II," *Burlington Magazine*, CVIII, 1966; J. A. Gere, *Taddeo Zuccaro*, Chicago, 1969.

T.M.D.

PALMA IL GIOVANE
Venice, 1544 (?) – Venice, 1628

11 STUDY FOR THE LAST JUDGMENT

Pen and brown ink and brown wash on blue paper; cropped on the left edge, vertical fold on the left, and laid down. 241 by 175 mm.; 9 7/16 by 6 7/8 in.

Blind stamp of the Russell Collection, Lugt 2648. Verso, in pencil, *J. Th* (John Thane, Lugt 1544).

PROVENANCE: W. Russell; Willette, 1808; W. Esdaile; J. Thane; A. Mathews (1959).

After the deaths of the sixteenth-century masters—Titian (d. 1576), Veronese (d. 1588), and Tintoretto (d. 1594)—Palma il Giovane was the leading Venetian painter. Palma was born into a family of artists, among whom were his father, a minor painter, and his great uncle, Palma Vecchio. The traditional birth date of 1544 is questionable, since Boschini and a signed self-portrait imply a date between 1548 and 1550 (Rosand, 1970, p. 149). Palma's early training was with his father. But in 1564 the Duke of Urbino called young Palma to study under his patronage. After three years Palma went to Rome, where he sketched works of Michelangelo, Raphael, and Polidoro da Caravaggio. He returned to Venice seeking commissions and was accepted into the artists' guild in 1575. Tintoretto had the greatest influence

on Palma's developing style in Venice. The two worked together redecorating the Venetian Ducal Palace which had been gutted by fire in both 1574 and 1577.

The *Study for the Last Judgment* represents Palma's early drawing style. It is on tinted Venetian paper and is drawn in ink, a medium favored by Palma. The drawing is very close to the signed study in the Uffizi (13088) for the painting, *Doge Pasquale Cicogna* (1585–95). Tintorettesque twisting figures, typical of Palma's early style, dominate both. Palma uses cross-hatching in each to model figures but also to create large areas of light and dark, supplementing the beautiful chiaroscuro of the washes. Not only is Palma's loose style present in both, but the same praying figure appears, as Palma often reused stock figures.

It has not been previously noticed that this drawing is a study for the painting of the *Last Judgment* in the Sala dello Scrutinio (1587–94) of the Ducal Palace. One other study is known (Tietze, no. 823, p. 199). The central grouping is clearly a study for the figure group in the lower left corner of the painting among the saved to the right of Christ. Palma drew lines on the drawing as guides for the edges of the painting. Various stages of development of the painting are visible on this sheet, from the original idea for an angel reaching down to save a soul to the final conception in the lower left of the drawing. The smaller scale of the drawing enabled Palma to avoid the overcrowding and lack of coherence he encountered in the painting in his unsuccessful attempt to emulate Tintoretto's massive *Paradise*, also in the Ducal Palace.

BIBLIOGRAPHY: Accademia Carrara di Bergamo, *Jacopo Palma il Giovane*, Bergamo, 1964; Gabinetto dei Disegni e delle Stampe, Uffizi, *Mostra di Disegni di Jacopo Palma il Giovane*, Florence, 1958; David Rosand, *Palma Giovane and Venetian Mannerism*, unpublished thesis for Columbia University, 1965; David Rosand, "Palma il Giovane as Draughtsman: the Early Career and Related Observations," *Master Drawings*, XIII, 1970; Hans Tietze and E. Tietze–Conrat, *The Drawings of the Venetian Painters*, New York, 1944; G. Gamulin, "Ritornando su Palma Giovane," *Arte Antica e Moderna*, 1961.

K.K.

PALMA IL GIOVANE
Venice, 1544 (?) – Venice, 1628

12 CHRIST HEALING THE BLIND MAN

Pen and brown ink, black chalk, brown and white wash, on buff paper; laid down. 132 by 227 mm.; 9 ⅛ by 5 ⅛ in.

Inscribed by the artist, *1623*. Mark of the Warwick Collection, Lugt 2600.

PROVENANCE: Earl of Warwick; C. R. Rudolph; A. Mathews (1962).

In the last thirty years of his life, Palma became the most sought-after painter in Venice. Palma and his studio were commissioned not only by the Venetian republic, churches, and confraternities, but by other patrons throughout Italy. Because of Palma's success, many of his later works reflect his increasing neglect of quality. His late works are also more classical as Palma attempted to tone down his twisting figures and to simplify the overcrowded designs of his earlier period. This classi-

cizing tendency is perhaps Palma's attempt to assimilate the new trends in Rome and Bologna.

Palma was always more interested in drawing than his older master, Tintoretto, whose drawings are studies and preparations for paintings. In the early seventeenth century, Palma and his contemporaries often drew for practice and relaxation alone. The Bick drawing is a good example of Palma's pen and wash drawings of this late period. It is a composition covering the full sheet and containing touches of white, so typical of Palma's late period. The composition is clearly ordered in simple rows of figures of the same height. Similar structure, feeling, and subject appear in many other late Palma drawings, such as the *Christ Consigning the Keys to Peter* in the Janos Schólz collection, dated 1625 (Muraro, p. 32), and *The Woman Taken in Adultery* in the National Gallery of Scotland, dated 1625 (Andrews, RSA 175).

But in the great quality and care with which *Christ Healing* is drawn, it is extremely close to Palma's late drawing, *The Taking of Christ*, in the Albertina (Stix, p. 97). The strength and sureness of each stroke and the vitality of the surfaces of light and dark in *Christ Healing* are unusual in Palma's late drawing.

In spite of its late style, *Christ Healing the Blind Man* has many similarities with the previous drawing, Palma's study for the *Last Judgment*. Within the more classical format of the later work, the figures, such as Christ, are still mannerist, serpentine forms. Details such as the hands, feet, and facial features are handled in much the same, and often clumsy, way in the two works. Palma uses a shorthand for these derived from his early contact with Tintoretto. Although his line is flowing in both, it rests on short strokes, often meaningless by themselves. The two drawings are excellent examples of Palma's early and late styles, respectively, as well as important documents of late Venetian Mannerism.

BIBLIOGRAPHY: Keith Andrews, *Catalogue of Italian Drawings*, Cambridge, 1968; The Arts Council, *Drawings from the C. R. Rudolph Collection*, London, 1961; Gabinetto dei Disegni e delle Stampe, Uffizi, *Mostra di Disegni di Jacopo Palma il Giovane*, Florence, 1958; Michelangelo Muraro, *Venetian Drawings from the Collection of Janos Schólz*, Venice, 1957; David Rosand, *Palma Giovane and Venetian Mannerism*, unpublished thesis for Columbia University, 1965; Alfred Stix and L. Fröhlich-Bum, *Beschreibender Katalog der Handzeichnungen*, I, Vienna, 1926; Hans Tietze and E. Tietze-Conrat, *The Drawings of the Venetian Painters*, New York, 1944.

K.K.

Follower of AGOSTINO CARRACCI
Bologna, 1557 – Rome, 1602

13 LANDSCAPE WITH FIGURES AND BIRDS

Pen and brown ink, touches of black chalk; laid down in a Richardson mat. Vertical center fold. 346 by 515 mm.; 13 ½ by 20 ⅜ in.

Blind stamp of the Richardson Collection, Lugt 2184; on the mount, mark of the Baskin Collection (pomegranate).

PROVENANCE: Jonathan Richardson, senior; Leonard Baskin; N. Chaikin.

13

This is a direct copy of a pen-and-ink drawing convincingly attributed to Agostino Carracci in the British Museum. The British Museum Agostino is torn into two sheets (inv. no. 1946–7–13–715, and 1951–5–5–1) which together measure 305 by 503 mm.—very close to the dimensions of the Bick drawing. The two drawings are similar in virtually every detail, but the London drawing must be considered the original, as the tight, wiry, energetic pen strokes testify. Agostino was primarily a printmaker and made ample use of parallel lines and cross-hatching in his work. Indeed, Wittkower attributes a somewhat pedantic cast in the drawings to these graphic devices.

Useful comparisons with the Bick drawing in determining the master's style are found in the Morgan Library sheet (Stampfle and Bean, no. 6), the Ellesmere *River Landscape with a Small Boat* (Mahon, no. 40), and the Albertina *Landscape with the Parable of the Good Samaritan* (Mahon no. 41). In all of these drawings the sheet is fragmented into a number of sections. In the Bick copy, this is particularly pronounced, as we find a large number of isolated figures, animals, and houses. In all four drawings, the backgrounds are elaborately finished, far more so than in the spare work of Agostino's brother, Annibale (in particular, the Louvre *Hanged Judas*). It is noteworthy, too, that the trees all suffer from a lack of firm structure. This is particularly true of the Bick copy and the Albertina work. In these, the trees seem almost reed-like. One might also note that all of the drawings seem to be characterized by a preoccupation with details.

It is possible that this work is from a series of the months, or of the trades (in this case, bird catching). An interesting sidelight is the volcano in the right background, a natural phenomenon for which there was something of a vogue among seventeenth- and eighteenth-century artists working in Italy.

BIBLIOGRAPHY: Keith Andrews, *National Gallery of Scotland, Catalogue of Italian Drawings,* Cambridge, 1968; Roseline Bacou, *Drawings in the Louvre: The Italian Drawings,* London, 1968; Denis Mahon, *Mostra dei Carracci,* Bologna, 1963; John Rupert Martin, *The Farnese Gallery,* Princeton, 1965; Juergen Schulz, *Master Drawings from California Collections,* Berkeley, 1968; Felice Stampfle and Jacob Bean, *Drawings from New York Collections II,* New York, 1967; Rudolf Wittkower, *The Drawings of the Carracci in the Collection of Her Majesty the Queen at Windsor Castle,* London, 1952.

R.H.L.

Attributed to CESARE POLLINI
Perugia, ca. 1560 – Perugia, ca. 1630

14 THE TRADES

Pen and brown ink. Watermark: bird in profile, on three balls, in a circle (Briquet, III, 12250). 141 by 237 mm.; 5 ½ by 9 5⁄16 in.

Inscribed with the names of the trades represented: *Tovagliaro; da panni; cimatori da lana; Pianellaro; Calzolaro; Peltraro; Pescatore; Ventagli e Ventoline; Battle l'Oro; Tripavo; Quel dall Ombrelle; Pasticcero; Limonaro; Scolari; Ottonaro; Dottore; Libraro*; inscribed, upper right, QUI SI SCRIVE MIMIA PRIVILEGI.

PROVENANCE: N. Chaikin.

This drawing belongs to a series of eight sheets representing the trades. Depicted here are activities which range from the marketing of umbrellas and fish to the profession of the scholar. Another drawing of similar size, style, and media is in the collection of Leonard Baskin, Northampton, Massachusetts, and appears to be the frontispiece of the series. Baskin's drawing is an allegory in which figures of Time, Honor, and Fame are represented, as well as a number of classical structures, raised, as an inscription tells us, to honor those who have been glorified for their achievements. The other six drawings of the series are in the art market, London.

The tradition of representing the trades is far from uncommon, even in late medieval art. In Italian printmaking it is exemplified by sets from the fifteenth century by the Master of the Planets, the sixteenth century by Domenico Beccafumi, and, roughly contemporary with the Bick drawing, by Guiseppe Maria Mitelli after Annibale Carracci. The format of these drawings, highly finished with careful inscriptions and an allegorical frontispiece, and the artist's use of an "engraved" crosshatching technique, strongly suggest that they were intended to be used for a series of prints, although such a series is not recorded by Bartsch.

The attribution of the drawing to Cesare Pollini, the Perugian draughtsman and miniaturist who did religious subjects and scenes of everyday life, was made (orally) by I. Fenyö. Two different yet not unrelated styles have already been attributed to Pollini: one often close to the sculptural manner of Baccio Bandinelli (Degenhart and Schmitt, no. 65; and Meder, p. 91, now in the Museum of Art, Rhode Island School of Design), and the other a freer, more mannerist style (Andrews, fig. 683, and Shickman, no. 26). The idea of a third style, characterized by a very careful touch and precise details, as found in the Bick drawing, is therefore not impossible. The strongest evidence for the attribution of this work to Pollini is a very small drawing (3 ½ by 4 ¾ in.), *Isaac, Rebecca, and Abimelech*, now in the New York art market. It is inscribed *Polloni* and is characterized by the same clear centralized space, doll-like figures, "engraved" cross-hatching, and straight parallel lines to define wall surfaces which are apparent in the Bick drawing. The New York drawing is also reminiscent of the other works given to Pollini. The striking differences among these three styles must restrain us from making a firm attribution to Pollini; in fact, Philip Pouncey, who has been responsible for the clarification of much of Pollini's work, has disagreed (by letter) with the attribution.

At the top right of the drawing is a figure looking through a telescope, which was invented in 1609, and thus provides a date before which the drawing could not have been done. The Munich drawings, close to Bandinelli in style, are more likely to have been done in the late sixteenth century, whereas the Bick and the New York drawings could well be a response to classical tendencies of the first half of the seventeenth century; the different function and degree of finish of the Bick drawing may also account for the changes in the artist's style.

BIBLIOGRAPHY: Keith Andrews, *National Gallery of Scotland, Catalogue of Italian Drawings*, Cambridge, 1968 (fig. 683); Adam Bartsch, *Le Peintre-Graveur*, Würzburg, 1920; Jacob Bean, *The Elsa Durand Mower Collection of French and Italian Drawings*, Princeton, 1968 (no. 35); Bernhart Degenhart and Annegrit Schmitt, *Italienische Zeichnungen 15.–18. Jahrhundert*, Munich, 1967 (no. 65); Joseph Meder, *Handzeichnungen Italienische Meister des XV–XVII Jahrhunderts*, Vienna, 1923 (p. 91); Lione Pascoli, *Vite De Pittori, Scultori, ed Architetti Perugini*, Amsterdam, 1965; H. Shickman Gallery, *Exhibition of Old Master Drawings*, New York, 1966 (no. 65). For photographic reproductions of other drawings by Pollini, see the Gernsheim archives.

K.L.G.

14

Attributed to PIETRO FACCINI

Bologna, 1562 – Bologna, 1602

15 MADONNA AND CHILD

Pen and brown ink with dark and light grey washes on light brown paper. Condition: torn into four pieces and then laid down; small paper losses. 170 by 146 mm.; 6⅝ by 5¾ in.

Lower left, monogram of Faccini (?). On mat, in pen and brown ink, *JB* (John Barnard, Lugt 1419).

PROVENANCE: J. Barnard.

Although Pietro Faccini studied in the workshop of the Carracci, he was drawn to the work of Baroccio and Correggio and also that of the Venetians. By the end of his career his style had matured to such a point that he could by no means be associated with the Bolognese school.

The drawing of the Madonna and Child in the clouds was deeply influenced by Federico Baroccio, one of the greatest masters of later Italian mannerism. Baroccio did an etching which can be dated no later than the 1570s, of the same subject as the Bick drawing and close to it in format. The etching later served as a source of inspiration for Jan Sadeler and even Rembrandt, who evidently owned a number of Baroccio's prints (Münz, II, p. 99).

The composition, motifs, and style of the etching and the Bick drawing are strongly similar. Faccini eliminated the two angels in the upper corners and changed the pose of the Virgin to a certain degree. However, the tilt of her head, her distinctively round face, and the position of the Child's legs have remained identical. In both the drawing and the etching the infant is clutching in his right hand some kind of fruit. Another convincing detail is the elaborate halo surrounding the heads of the Madonna and Child.

A comparison with other paintings and drawings of the Madonna and Child given to Faccini shows a similar dependence on Baroccio's prototypes, for example, *The Virgin and Child and St. Dominic* and *The Mystery of the Rosary* in the Parish Church, Quarto Inferiore, *The Mystic Marriage of St. Catherine*, Melinari-Pradelli collection, Bologna, and a drawing of the *The Virgin and Child with the Saints*, in the British Museum.

BIBLIOGRAPHY: Ludwig Münz, *The Etchings of Rembrandt*, New York, 1954; Harold Olsen, *Baroccio*, Copenhagen, 1962; A. Venturi, *Storia dell'Arte Italiana*, IX, 7, Milan, 1933.

T.M.D.

15

GUGLIELMO CACCIA, IL MONCALVO

Montabone, 1568 – Moncalvo, 1625

16 NOAH AND HIS FAMILY PREPARING TO ENTER THE ARK

Black chalk, red chalk, pen and brown ink; horizontal center fold. The composition is within an oval (in black chalk). 380 by 295 mm.; 15 by 11 ⅞ in.

Watermark: three circles arranged vertically; in the middle circle possibly a fish (dolphin).

PROVENANCE: A. L. de Mestral de Saint Saphorin; R. de Cérenville; N. Chaikin.

Guglielmo Caccia, better known as Il Moncalvo, studied first under Lombard masters, yet little is known of their identity. By 1593 the artist was working in Moncalvo where he remained, except for short periods, until his death in 1625. Moncalvo later studied under Bernardino Lanino and was influenced throughout his career by both Leonardo and Correggio, whose style was brought to Lombardy by other masters.

This late mannerist drawing, a scene from the story of Noah and the ark, is undoubtedly from the hand of Moncalvo. In the foreground the artist has presented a dramatic figure of a grateful Noah (lower left) in the company of his wife and offspring. Directly above these figures are the various pairs of animals preparing to enter the ark. Above this, the drawing has been completed only in black and red chalk without the outline of pen and ink of the lower half. Nevertheless, on close examination other human figures are visible (upper left) and represent, most likely, Noah and his family already in the ark. In the top of the composition God the Father looms out of the sky giving further instructions to a kneeling Noah.

Stylistically, our drawing is typical of Moncalvo's work. For example, a drawing of two women by Moncalvo (*Italian 16th Century Drawings*, no. 45) shows a figure with the same tilt of the head, crossed arms, and graceful sway of the body that are present in a female figure in the Bick drawing. Another element of style that is most characteristic of Moncalvo is the use of very short repetitive strokes in the modeling of the figure. This is clear in the putti of our drawing and can be compared to another drawing by the artist in the Accademia Carrara, Bergamo. In both works the short modeling strokes almost seem to outline parts of the figure.

Since the figures have been placed within an oval, the drawing may have been a preliminary sketch for the decoration of a church or private palace.

BIBLIOGRAPHY: Ivan Fenyö, *Northern Italian Drawings*, New York, 1965; A. Venturi, *Storia dell'Arte Italiana*, IX, 7, Milan, 1933; Keith Andrews, *National Gallery of Scotland, Catalogue of Italian Drawings*, Cambridge, 1968; *Italian 16th Century Drawings*, Scottish Arts Council, Edinburgh, 1969.

T.M.D.

16

Anonymous Venetian, late sixteenth century

17 MINIATURE FROM THE COMMISSION TO DANIEL, PODESTÀ OF TREVISO

Tempera on vellum. 209 by 153 mm.; 8 ¼ by 6 in.

Verso, inscribed in pen and ink in another hand, *3*; in pen and ink, as part of the *Ducale*, NOS MARINUS / GRIMANO / DEI GR [ATI] A DUX / VENETIAR [UM] ETC. / COMMETTEMO / ATE NOBEL HOMO DANIEL / *Diletto Cittadin et fedel nostro, che* / *in nome di Giesu Christo vadi* [?] *et* / *sij* [sic] *Podesta et capitanio de nostro* / *mandato della Citta di Treviso* / *per mesi sedeci et tanto piú* [sic], *grias-* / *to differira il tuo successore a ve-* / *nire Havendo di detta terra buona* / *et diligente cura per honor nostro* / *et per il buon stato, et conserva-* / *tione di essa, governando Nostra* [?] / *citta in quelle cose, che a be*[n] *spettarano* / *secondo le consuetudini, et statuti*

PROVENANCE: A. Caselli (1968).

This miniature is taken from a Venetian *Ducale*, one of the most important sources of Venetian illumination from the middle fifteenth to the eighteenth century. The term *Ducale* includes covenants which the Duke of Venice made with the people, congratulatory addresses, and ducal commissions. The Bick miniature is the frontispiece from one of the commissions, which were books of local laws especially prepared in the name of the Duke for new mayors of each of the cities in the Venetian Republic. According to the inscription on the verso, the *Commission* was given to Daniel, appointed Mayor and Captain of Treviso by Duke Marino Grimani (1595–1605) for sixteen months; Daniel is told to govern well, according to established customs and statutes. The one hundred or more pages which once followed our miniature recorded the laws of Treviso for the new mayor. Daniel appears on the recto in contemporary dress receiving the commission; perhaps his son is next to him. St. Mark, with his symbol the lion, is above Daniel. Christ, holding the banner of the Resurrection, St. Sebastian, with two arrows, and St. Roch, with a pilgrim's hat, appear together as protectors against the plague. These three appear in a similar way in the famous *Mariegola dei Calafati* in the Museo Correr (Bratti, 2, p. 179), done after the great plague of 1576 in Venice. At the top of the frame is the winged lion, symbol of Venice, and probably, at the bottom center, the coat of arms of Daniel formerly appeared. Six partially erased female allegorical figures appear on the sides, with a bow, with a bird or chalice, with arms outstretched, and with a wheel (?).

Because it was executed for Grimani, the miniature can be dated between 1595 and 1605. Stylistically, it belongs in the late sixteenth century (Bratti, 1907, pp. 187–199). Few names of possible illuminators are known. Gasparo of Verona, Giorgio Colonna, and Alessandro Merli are among the most significant illuminators of the various preserved *Ducali*. A signed Gasparo page in the Pierpont Morgan Library (M353), which is also close to a miniature in Dublin (Sutton, p. 12), is stylistically much more mannerist than ours. The Bick drawing has been attributed to Merli, but his signed miniatures (Hermitage; Marciana Library 1350–8085) are

17

different in style from ours, freer in brush work and in the placing of figures in space. The possibility of a youthful work cannot be excluded since Merli worked in Venice in 1590, ten years before his datable commission, and several earlier and tighter works have been attributed to him with some hesitation (Fenyö, p. 40; Gukovsky, p. 220). Colonna's signed miniature in the *Mariegola dei Calafati* was done in 1577–78; the much greater interest in volumes, and the crowding of figures in our own miniature, as well as other stylistic differences, indicate a hand other than Colonna's. The artist of the present work must be placed somewhere between Colonna and Merli in time and style.

BIBLIOGRAPHY: Erhard Aeschlimann and Paolo d'Ancona, *Dictionnaire des Miniaturistes*, Milan, 1949; Paolo d'Ancona, *La Miniature Italienne*, Paris, 1925; Ricciotti Bratti, "Arte Retrospectiva: Miniature Veneziane," *Emporium*, xxv, 1907; Ricciotti Bratti, "La *Mariegola* dei Calafati dell'Arsenale di Venezia," *Dedalo*, 2, 1921–22; David Diringer, *The Illuminated Book*, New York, 1967; Ivan Fenyö, *Disegni Veneti del Museo di Budapest*, Venice, 1965; Matteo Gukovsky, "Un Manoscritto Veneziano del Secolo XVI nella Biblioteca dell'Ermitage di Leningrad," *Arte Veneta*, 1969; Giulia Maria Zuccolo Padrona, "Postilla Attorno ad Alessandro Merli," *Arte Veneta*, 1969; Larissa Salmina, *Disegni Veneti del Museo di Leningrad*, Venice, 1964; Denys Sutton, *Drawings from the National Gallery of Ireland*, New York, 1967; L. Testi, *La Storia della Pittura Veneziana*, Bergamo, 1909.

K.K.

Anonymous, seventeenth-century Roman-Bolognese

18 HEAD OF A MAN

Black and white chalk on brown paper; laid down. 265 by 183 mm.; 10½ by 7¼ in.

PROVENANCE: A. Caselli (1968).

Full-page heads of bearded old men of this type were so popular with the Roman-Bolognese classicists of the early seventeenth century that it is almost impossible to determine to which of several artists this head should be assigned. The pose, as well as the cold, smooth, reflective surface, indicate that it might have been drawn after the Laocoön, a sculpture unearthed in 1506 and used as a model by many Renaissance and Baroque artists.

The quality of line here—the hatching used to model the cheeks and forehead, the ebullient curls—and the strong diagonal movement suggest Guido Reni as a possible source. Figures which seem very similar, when the smudged condition of the Bick drawing is taken into account, appear in three Uffizi drawings, *Study for a Virgin of the Assumption*, *Head of a Saint*, and *Head of an Old Man*. The luminosity and ethereal quality of the work, however, suggest the possibility that the drawing might even be French.

P.C.S.

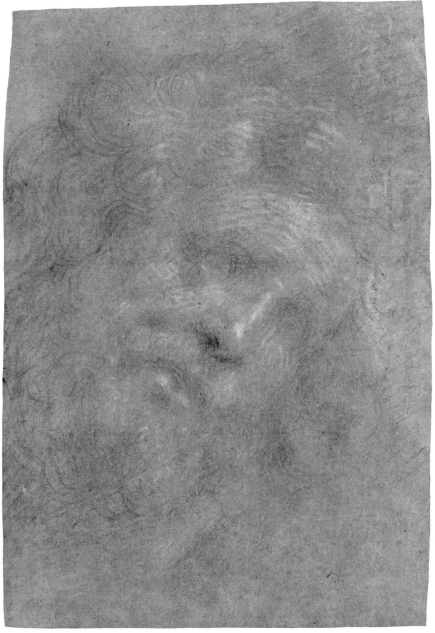

18

Anonymous, seventeenth-century Roman-Bolognese

19 HEAD OF A MAN

> Black and white chalk on grey paper; clipped at all four corners. 360 by 242 mm.; 14 ¼ by 9 ½ in.

> Verso, in an old hand, in pen and brown ink, *Da Barth. o Schedoni Modaneso . . .* Another attribution to Schedoni has been inscribed on a piece of paper pasted to the mount.

> PROVENANCE: A. Caselli (1968).

This drawing is attributed to Bartolomeo Schedoni (1570–1615) in two inscriptions in fairly modern hands; the monumentality, structural quality, and emotional subtlety of this head suggest that it is a study for the central figure of a canvas, and this author could locate no such painting by Schedoni. Several drawings, such as a *St. Paul*, Parma, Galleria Nazionale, contain similar faces of less prominence. The facial type, style of drawing and format, more than filling the page, are typical of many artists of the period besides Schedoni, especially Roman-Bolognese artists of the seventeenth century. Just as close, for example, are figures in Domenichino's decoration of the apse and crossing of S. Andrea della Valle, as well as many of his well-known sketches of old men.

The influence of Guido Reni is also a strong possibility, as in his series of the four evangelists, Bob Jones University, Greenville, though sources might well be found in sixteenth-century Venetian draughtsmanship as well. In short, while the inscribed attribution to Schedoni is not impossible, the stylistic evidence points no more strongly to him than to Domenichino or several other artists.

P.C.S.

OTTAVIO LEONE

Rome, ca. 1578 – Rome, 1630

20 PORTRAIT OF A MAN

> Black, white and red chalk on faded blue paper. 235 by 162 mm.; 9 ¼ by 6 ⅜ in.

> In pen and brown ink, *304 setenbre; 1624.* Verso, in pen and brown ink, *62; S. Franc. Tenturcine* (or *Centurcine*).

> PROVENANCE: Samuel Newbury; N. Chaikin.

Ottavio Leone was portraitist to several courts throughout Italy, as well as in Rome, and drew the full spectrum of court life, from Pope Gregory XV to artist and musician friends. His way of suggestively drawing out the image towards the edges of the paper with quick strokes and sfumato effects, and then making the lines progressively darker and firmer towards the eyes at the center, which are very

19

clear and penetrating, gave his drawings a psychological force which made them extremely popular.

Who numbered, dated, and inscribed in pen and ink the series of Leone drawings of which this is a part is not clear. Prince Borghese reportedly owned more than 400 Leone portraits, seen in Paris in 1747, and dispersed after the death of the last owner, M. d'Aubigny (Parker, p. 450). Certainly, such precise dating and identification could only be done by the artist, or a collector very close to the artist.

The meaning of the number "304" over the month, September, has not been definitely determined. A portrait of Cardinal Francesco Barberini, in colored chalk on similar paper, in the British Museum, bears the inscription, *305 setenbre 1624*, and a portrait of Conte Filippo Spinola, in black, white, and red chalk on blue paper, in the National Gallery of Canada, is inscribed *302 setenbre 1624*. An investigation of some seventy of these drawings shows a relation between the numbers and the dates, indicating that the drawings were numbered as they were dated, over a period of at least fifteen years. The lowest number recorded appears to be 6, from January, 1615, in the Hamburg Kunsthalle; drawings from 1614 and earlier do not seem to be numbered. The highest number of the series found is 434, September, 1629, in the Pierpont Morgan Library (*Drawings from New York Collections II*, no. 27), and there appear to be only two Leone drawings dated after 1615 not numbered in sequence: a portrait of a man in the Albertina catalogued as 334, May, 1620, but whose date is not visible in reproduction, and another portrait, of indifferent quality, in the Meisner collection, numbered (in a slightly different hand) *10 marzo 1632*, two years after Leone's death.

All the numbered drawings examined are on light blue paper of approximately the same size, suggesting a notebook, or at least a coherent series. Only three drawings dated after 1614 known to this writer do not have numbers, at Edinburgh, at the École des Beaux-Arts, Paris, and in the Ashmolean Museum. Only one drawing, an unnumbered and undated portrait of a man in the Albertina, is not on bluish paper, allowing for aging and stains.

Leandro Bassano's chalk drawings, again often on typical Venetian blue paper, are close to Leone's work; an artist of the next generation, the Venetian Sebastiano Bombelli, seems aware of Leone's portrait drawings.

There is another Leone in the Bick collection, a portrait of a man, from the Abbott collection (Lugt 970).

BIBLIOGRAPHY: Keith Andrews, *National Gallery of Scotland, Catalogue of Italian Drawings*, Cambridge, 1968; Roberto Longhi, *Paragone*, 1951, no. 21, p. 36; K. T. Parker, *Catalogue of Drawings in the Ashmolean Museum*, II, Oxford, 1956; A. E. Popham and K. M. Fenwick, *European Drawings from the National Gallery of Canada*, Ottawa, 1969; Felice Stampfle and Jacob Bean, *Drawings from New York Collections II*, New York, 1967; A. Stix and L. Fröhlich-Bum, *Beschreibender Katalog der Handzeichnungen*, I, III, Vienna, 1926.

P.C.S.

304
setunbre

1624

20

FRANCESCO GRIGIOTTI

flourished, Rome, 1604–1635

21 ST. JEROME IN PENITENCE

Pen and brown ink, sometimes retouched in pencil, blue wash, on vellum; laid down. The ink has faded in a number of places. 261 by 357 mm.; 10 ¼ by 14 in.

Inscribed by the artist in pen and brown ink: *Franc. Grigiotis fece di / Decemb. 1623 in Ro.a / Roma relicta solus in sylvis ago / Hic Roma tamen est; et puellarum choris / Intersum Eremi cultor. Haud fugi satis / Urbem sequacem. Me cavernis inferam / Si forte Roma his concidat . . . alis.* Mark of the Huart Collection (?), Lugt 2084. Mount, verso: in pencil, *Great St. Jerome Agostino Carracci drawing on vellum by Francesco Brizzi* (crossed out), *dated 1623 Grigiotti*; mark of the Ingram Collection, Lugt 1405a; unidentified mark (CW?).

PROVENANCE: P. Huart (?); B. Ingram; A. Caselli (1968).

Francesco Grigiotti, a seventeenth-century Italian illuminator, worked in Rome from 1604 to 1635, when he painted a missal for Pope Urban VIII. Although little is known about Grigiotti, examples of his work can be found in the Cathedral of Toledo. A small miniature of the *Flight into Egypt*, a gift of Urban VIII to his brother Don Carlo Barberini, is also known to be from his hand.

Our drawing shows a naked, bearded figure of a man crouching at the entrance to a cave. Inside a straw hut to the side of the cave can be seen an open book and a standing crucifix which, along with the lion in the foreground and the landscape setting, identify the subject as St. Jerome repenting in the wilderness. The inscription confirms this identification and connects the drawing with a particular legend associated with St. Jerome. Its translation reads: "With Rome left behind I wander alone in the forests. Yet Rome is here; and as a caretaker of the desert, I am amongst choirs of girls. I have not completely fled from the city that pursues me. I shall bring myself to the caverns to see if by chance Rome . . . should fall." The life of St. Jerome tells us that while a priest in Rome, St. Jerome openly criticized the loose and lavish life of some of the clerks and monks, and then was mocked and scorned by them until he felt forced to leave Rome and suffer for Christ's sake in the desert. In a treatise on virginity which he wrote to Eustochium, daughter of St. Paula (Letter XXII, section 7), St. Jerome related how in the desert he fancied himself to be back among the pleasures of Rome. Yet in spite of his fasting and humiliation, he was constantly obsessed with lewd dreams of dancing naked girls. Angry with his thoughts, he beat his breast with a stone and prayed for peace of mind and flesh. He remained in the desert for four years until his penance was accomplished.

The style and composition of this drawing bring to mind the landscape drawings of various Netherlandish artists of the early years of the seventeenth century. Dated 1623, the drawing was done during the years when Grigiotti was known to have been working in Rome. Many Northern artists were also in Rome at this time, and it is possible that Grigiotti was influenced by their styles. The function of this drawing, which, like many works on vellum, has faded in several places, is difficult to determine; although the presence of the inscription suggests that it may have been

21

P H

intended for a print, its highly finished character and the fact that it was done on vellum indicate that it may have been a drawing commissioned and sold for itself.

BIBLIOGRAPHY: F. S. Ellis (ed.), *The Golden Legend*, v, London, 1900; U. Thieme and F. Becker, *Allgemeines Lexikon der Bildenden Künstler*, xv, Leipzig, 1922; F. A. Wright, *Select Letters of St. Jerome*, London, 1933.

K.L.G.

GIOVANNI FRANCESCO BARBIERI, IL GUERCINO
Cento, 1591 – Bologna, 1666

22 MAN IN PROFILE TO THE LEFT, HOLDING A BOOK

Pen and dark brown ink. 202 by 172 mm.; 8 by 6¾ in.

PROVENANCE: A. Mathews (1959).

The present work can be compared to a striking drawing by Guercino in the Fogg Museum of a somewhat analogous subject, *Man Sitting at a Table Reading* (Mongan and Sachs, no. 263). There are strong stylistic similarities in the rendering of the heads; both effectively create contrasts with the dark ink and use dots to form facial features. In the Fogg drawing, the artist works in a freer manner, particularly in the washes and the loose, fluent line. The Bick drawing is characterized by a harder line in general, although the figure's barely suggested right arm, and the way it ends off the page, are masterful in their freedom.

The confusion involved in accurately identifying a drawing by Guercino is due to the large number of his followers and able imitators who worked during the seventeenth and eighteenth centuries. A landscape drawing in the Bick collection by the eighteenth-century artist Palmieri (no. 45) exemplifies the Guercino vogue excellently. Even a drawing of a seated youth by Sir Joshua Reynolds in the John Nicholas Brown collection, Providence, is a direct copy of a Guercino of the same size and medium in the Mahon collection, London (*Omaggio al Guercino*, no. 45).

There are also problems involved in dating a drawing by Guercino, for he is known to have imitated his own earlier style. When Guercino was asked in 1660 by Don Antonio Ruffo to do a companion piece to Rembrandt's *Aristotle Contemplating the Bust of Homer* in his earlier "broad manner," he promptly replied that in order to harmonize with the Rembrandt, he was quite willing to paint "della mia prima maniera gagliarda" (Held, p. 5).

The Bick drawing is certainly of the same outstanding quality of other works convincingly attributed to Guercino. The striking difference between this drawing and that of the following work, from later in Guercino's career, shows the influence of Roman-Bolognese classicism in his growing refinement of line and chiaroscuro.

BIBLIOGRAPHY: Jacob Bean and Felice Stampfle, *Drawings from New York Collections II*, 1967; A. DeWitt, *Incisioni Italiane del Quattrocento*, Florence, 1963; Julius Held, *Rembrandt's Aristotle*

22

and Other Rembrandt Studies, Princeton, 1969; Denis Mahon, Il Guercino – Catalogo Critico dei Disegni, 1968; Denis Mahon, Omaggio al Guercino, 1967; Agnes Mongan and Paul J. Sachs, Drawings in the Fogg Museum of Art, Cambridge, 1940; J. Rosenberg, "Rembrandt and Guercino," Art Quarterly, 1944; A. Stix and L. Fröhlich-Bum, Beschreibender Katalog der Handzeichnungen, I, Vienna, 1926.

S.K.H.

GIOVANNI FRANCESCO BARBIERI, IL GUERCINO
Cento, 1591 – Bologna, 1666

23 PUTTO WITH GRAPES

Red chalk; repaired, lower left corner. 280 by 205 mm.; 11 by 8 ⅛ in.

Verso, in pencil, Guerchino.

PROVENANCE: art market, London; N. Chaikin.

Both the subject and the style of this drawing suggest Guercino's later period at Bologna, 1642–66. His works grow calmly classical and smoothly finished in these last years, in sharp contrast to his strongly Caravaggesque phase in the second and third decades of the century. For example, The Virgin and Child with a Book and a Pot of Pinks by Guercino at the Pierpont Morgan Library (Bean and Stampfle, no. 47) has been dated at the beginning of this later Bolognese period. There is a striking similarity in the handling of the red chalk and in the anatomy and pose of the Christ Child and putto, though there is less smudging of the line to render contrasts in the Bick drawing.

Another work, two studies of the crucified Christ in the Denis Mahon collection, London (Omaggio al Guercino, no. 149), is a study for a painting done ca. 1644 in the Chiesa del Rosario, Cento, and is close to the present drawing in its refined and finished delicacy of touch. In contrast to these works is an earlier drawing at the Metropolitan Museum in New York, Standing Boy Holding a Bowl (Bean and Stampfle, no. 46) where Guercino's use of the chalk during his middle period can be seen.

Charles Dempsey has pointed out (by letter) that the iconographic use of amorini to personify the seasons is a common one in the seventeenth and eighteenth centuries, for example, in paintings by Albani and Maratti. The prototypes of this theme are Hellenistic and Roman, and the reason for the use of Amors in such personifications has to do with the iconography of Venus and her role as leader of the Graces and the Hours, and hence the seasons. Two fifteenth-century works, a woodcut in the Hypnerotomachia Poliphili of 1499 and an engraving, The Vintage of the Cupids, ca. 1465–70, by an anonymous Florentine (DeWitt, no. VI), are similar in theme. Hind reproduces no less than four fifteenth-century Italian engravings showing this subject. In the late sixteenth century, Annibale Carracci made several wash drawings for engravings on silver of The Drunken Silenus in which he used the motif of putti with grape arbor and baskets (Burlington Magazine, XCVII, 1955, pp. 282–287).

23

That Guercino turned to this subject more than once is seen in a black-and-red chalk drawing of four children around a tub, holding grapes and jugs, in the Chatsworth Collection. It is very similar in dimensions to the Bick drawing (206 by 297 mm.). There is also a variation of this theme in pen and ink done in Guercino's style by a later hand (Francesco Bartolozzi?) in the Albertina (no. 446).

S.K.H.

REMIGIO CANTAGALLINA
flourished, Florence, 1582 – 1635

24 VILLAGE SCENE

Pen and brown ink, black chalk, brown wash; laid down on canvas and partially removed. Repairs on left side of the paper. Watermark: hat, with two tassels on cords hanging down from inside it and draped in decorative patterns around a three-humped mountain design within an oval. 205 by 329 mm.; 8 1/16 by 12 15/16 in.

Verso, in black chalk, R. CANTAGALLINA; *no. 650—*.

PROVENANCE: A. Mathews (1961).

Remigio Cantagallina is an example of an artist who has become known almost solely through his drawings. Although he executed many prints and did drawings of individual figures, it is his many landscape drawings, characterized by an intimate feeling for contemporary life and trees with lively, twisting trunks and tightly defined clusters of leaves, that have given him a place among the more important Florentine artists of the early seventeenth century. His landscapes show a close affinity with the work of Jacques Callot, Stefano della Bella (nos. 27 and 28), Ercole Bazzicaluva, and Giulio Parigi; typical of many drawings from this group of artists are a pen line and cross-hatching reminiscent of engravings and échoppe etchings. Cantagallina may well have been something of an amateur artist, since it seems that he was also an engineer.

Although the present drawing, a charming document of the everyday activity in a small Italian town, does not show Cantagallina at his most vigorous or incisive, it is, nevertheless, typical of many scenes attributed to the master, the closest of which is a drawing given to the artist and dated 1633 in the Art Museum, Princeton (Bean, no. 32). Both drawings use the natural variety of architectural forms—porticoes, arcades, steps, half-ruined walls—to relieve any feeling of strictness in the construction of the space of the village square, which is very centrally placed on the sheet and clearly defined in the essentials of its construction. Rather than dominating this architecture, the figures carry on their activities within it. Other drawings of village squares include one in the Uffizi and another in the Julius Held collection, New York (Vitzthum, p. 556), both of which show the Fair at Impruneta, the subject of one of Callot's most magnificent etchings. The date on the Princeton draw-

ing may not be conclusive in determining Cantagallina's chronology, since another drawing of a little town, with an artist and a dog in the foreground, in the same media, and in much the same style, is dated 1616 (Boerner, p. 117, no. 501).

BIBLIOGRAPHY: Jacob Bean, *Italian Drawings in the Art Museum, Princeton University*, New York, 1966; C. G. Boerner, *Graphik und Handzeichnungen*, Düsseldorf, 1959; Walter Vitzthum, "Drawings from the Collection of Julius Held," *Burlington Magazine*, CXII, 1970.

B. W.

REMIGIO CANTAGALLINA
flourished, Florence, 1582 – 1635

25 LANDSCAPE

Pen and brown ink, brown wash, black chalk, border in brown ink; laid down. Vertical center fold. Watermark: double circle; otherwise illegible. 257 by 385 mm.; 10 by 13 ¼ in.

PROVENANCE: H. Wellesley; D. Kelly; H. Calmann (1960).

Although such a dramatic view of a bridge seems to be unusual in Cantagallina's work, the delight in architecture for its own sake and particularly the love for tunnels and arches, here allowed full play, is characteristic of this simple, direct artist. For example, in Edinburgh (Andrews, RSA 138) there is another drawing by the artist which shows a deep tunnel through a hillside; in the lower left, a dog like the one in the present drawing faces head down toward the bottom of the sheet. It is in drawings like these that one feels most strongly Cantagallina's affinity for northern, particularly Netherlandish, landscape draughtsmen, several of whom worked in Rome, such as Paul Bril (Bernt, I, nos. 128–130), the Valckenborch's, and Jan Brueghel (see his drawings of the waterfall at Tivoli in the Rijksprentenkabinet, Amsterdam, the Prentenkabinet, Leiden, and the Louvre). However, such a scene is certainly not uncommon in the milieu in which Cantagallina worked, as shown in an etching of this subject by Callot (Lieure, II, no. 259).

This drawing has the same provenance as a *Street Scene* in the Ashmolean Museum and a *Stigmatization of St. Francis* of 1615 in the Janos Scholz collection (*Italian Landscape Drawings . . .*, no. 9). The catalogue of the Ashmolean collection (p. 568) notes that the Oxford sheet is from a set of 105 drawings, evidently mostly by Cantagallina, sold in London in 1954 and inscribed *Vedute di Toscana d'Jacopo Ligozzi*, of which the Bick drawing appears to have been a part.

BIBLIOGRAPHY: Keith Andrews, *National Gallery of Scotland, Catalogue of Italian Drawings*, Cambridge, 1968; Walther Bernt, *Die Niederländischen Zeichner des 17. Jahrhunderts*, Munich, 1957; J. Lieure, *Jacques Callot*, Paris, 1929; K. T. Parker, *Catalogue of the Collection of Drawings in the Ashmolean Museum*, II, Oxford, 1956; Duke University, *Italian Landscape Drawings from the Collection of Janos Scholz*, Durham, 1965.

B. W.

25

GIOVANNI FRANCESCO GRIMALDI

Bologna, 1606 – Rome, 1680

26 LANDSCAPE WITH FIGURES AND BUILDINGS AND A BOAT

VERSO: BATHERS IN A LANDSCAPE.

Pen and brown ink, touches of black chalk. 207 by 312 mm.; 8 3/16 by 12 5/16 in.

Lower left, in the artist's hand, 5. Marks of the Johnstone Collection, Lugt 2608a, and the Houlditch Collection, Lugt 2214.

PROVENANCE: R. Houlditch; W. B. Johnstone; A. Caselli (1968).

Giovanni Francesco Grimaldi, a relative of the Carracci, studied at their famous school in Bologna, and also studied with Francesco Albani. In 1626, he went to Rome, where he became the architect and painter of two successive popes, Urban VIII and Innocent X. In 1649, Grimaldi, with the painter Romanelli, was called to Paris by Cardinal Mazarin in order to decorate the Cardinal's palace (now the Bibliothèque Nationale). While in Paris, Grimaldi also decorated the apartments occupied by Anne of Austria in the Louvre. In 1651, he returned to Rome where he immediately reestablished his reputation, and did considerable work for Pope Alexander VII and Pope Clement IX. He was also president of the Academy of St. Luke at this time and died, very popular, at the age of 74. In addition to the work in Paris and the papal work, Grimaldi also executed four large landscapes for the Borghese Palace.

Grimaldi was also a brilliant etcher and nearly all of his drawings bear witness to this fact. While the drawings may not be preparatory studies for etchings, there can be little doubt that the hand that maneuvers the etching needle maneuvers the pen in a roughly similar fashion. The Bick Grimaldi manifests these etching-like characteristics in the shading and in the lightness of the background. The foreground is much darker, as though it had been "bitten" twice by the etching acid.

Grimaldi was attracted to river landscapes—indeed, they are a favorite subject. A stunning example of his affinity for such scenes is the drawing in the Metropolitan (Stampfle and Bean, no. 80), which, incidentally, exhibits to a high degree the etching-like techniques previously mentioned. Although the Bick drawing is not of the same quality as this masterpiece, it is quite similar to other Grimaldi river scenes in Edinburgh, the British Museum, the Royal Library at Windsor Castle, and the Gabinetto Nazionale delle Stampe in Rome.

BIBLIOGRAPHY: Keith Andrews, *National Gallery of Scotland, Catalogue of Italian Drawings*, Cambridge, 1968; K. T. Parker, *Catalogue of Drawings in the Ashmolean Museum*, Oxford, 1956; *Handzeichnungen Alter Meister aus Schweitzer Privatbesitz*, Zürich, 1967; Felice Stampfle and Jacob Bean, *Drawings from New York Collections II*, New York, 1967.

R.H.L.

Giovanni Francesco Grimaldi
26 *verso:* BATHERS IN A LANDSCAPE

STEFANO DELLA BELLA

Florence, 1610 – Florence, 1664

27 LANDSCAPE WITH BUILDINGS AND HORSEMAN

Pen and brown ink; laid down. Repaired, lower right; foxing. 77 by 162 mm.;
3 1/16 by 6 3/8 in.

In pencil, *10*; in pen and black ink, *Stefanino*. On the back of the mount, in black chalk: *B 187*; *St. della Bella*; *B240*; *16105*.

PROVENANCE: A. Mathews (1957).

Stefano della Bella was trained as both a goldsmith and painter before he finally settled on a career as a draughtsman and engraver. From 1633 to 1639 he visited Rome, in which period the works of Callot—whom Stefano discovered at a very early age—exerted their strongest influence. In 1639, della Bella left for Paris where, by 1645, his style underwent a definite change. Imitation of Callot gave way to the influence of several Dutch artists, such as Both, Breenbergh, Swanevelt, and Rembrandt—whose works he had an opportunity to study first-hand during a trip to Holland in 1647. Around 1649 della Bella executed various costume and ballet series which show the *petit-maître* at his most inventive and fantastic best. By 1650, a year after his return to Florence, his style appears to change once again: his lines become freer, less fastidious, less mannered. This final period is characterized by something of a decline in the artist's inventiveness, due in part, it would seem, to the decline in general of artistic enthusiasm in the Florence of that time.

Stefano's precise niche in the history of art is difficult to determine. His mannerist delicacy, his pronounced bent for ornament and the macabre, above all the inscrutability of his outlook make proper assessment, especially in our present age, difficult. Nonetheless, it cannot be denied that at times he is a first-rate draughtsman and often displays remarkable subtlety of observation.

Landscapes of the general type of our drawing were far from uncommon with the Italian followers of Callot, most especially with such artists as Ercole Bazzicaluva, Sinibaldo Scorza, and Remigio Cantagallina (nos. 24, 25). Indeed, this drawing seems even a step closer to Callot by virtue of the parallel penstrokes, seen most clearly in the left foreground and in the building in shadow. The peculiar quality of the lines in our drawing, varying in width but with clear divisions between one width and another, suggests a conscious attempt to recapture the controlled, yet strangely kinetic quality of a line created by the échoppe—an etching tool often used by Callot with a point with faces of different width which could be alternated to create a swelling and tapering line.

On the other hand, our drawing presents certain stylistic problems. The artist's handling of space is here already far closer to the work of various Dutch landscapists such as Swanevelt and Breenbergh. Imitation of Callot's uninterrupted planes of forms have seemingly given way to the rather dramatic use of empty but expressive spaces, a characteristic typically Dutch. The repoussoir at left, for instance, and its almost ambiguous relation to the middle-ground exemplifies the change of attitude. Nonetheless, for all the delicacy of Stefano's treatment, there is a certain tightness of

composition and outline that seems rather uncharacteristic as yet of the freedom and fluency that is associated with his Dutch phase. It would appear then that this drawing represents a transition of sorts between two artistic phases: while his abandonment of Callot is far from complete on the one hand, della Bella already incorporates some of the Dutch elements that were to influence him so profoundly in the subsequent phase of his development.

BIBLIOGRAPHY: Anthony Blunt, *The Drawings of G. B. Castiglione and Stefano della Bella at Windsor Castle*, London, 1954; Eckhart Knab, *Jacques Callot und sein Kreis*, Vienna, 1969; J. Lieure, *Jacques Callot*, Paris, 1929; Daniel Ternois, *L'Art de Jacques Callot*, Paris, 1962; Alexandre de Vesme, *Le Peintre-Graveur Italien*, Milan, 1906.

U.B.

STEFANO DELLA BELLA
Florence, 1610 – Florence, 1664

28 COSTUME FIGURE

VERSO: three female figures in voluminous dress, cut off at the neck by the top (recto, left) edge.

Pen and brown ink; laid down on an old mount with a border in pen and brown ink. Watermark of the mount: a sun with a smiling face and eight rays; beneath it, an H. 200 by 86 mm.; 7 7/8 by 3 7/16 in.

PROVENANCE: Kinnaird Castle; A. Mathews (1960).

Around 1650 Stefano did a series of costume, ballet, and *feste* drawings. All of these were done in watercolors, and display a remarkable lightness of touch and a high degree of imagination, even fantasy. It is believed that della Bella may have made a trip to the East during this period; our drawing, furthermore, is most probably an "oriental costume," and perhaps an intended preliminary sketch for one of the above-mentioned costume series. In any event, it is likely that our drawing is a trimmed-down leaf of a sketchbook. It is thought that one or more sketchbooks, each varying in subject matter and sizes, were cut up and assembled into one album —the so-called "Kinnaird Castle Album"—and later broken up and sold as individual drawings, of which ours is an example. The distinctive watermark of the mount, described above, may be helpful in determining the identity of the drawings that formed this album.

BIBLIOGRAPHY: Anthony Blunt, *The Drawings of G. B. Castiglione and Stefano della Bella at Windsor Castle*, London, 1954; Alexandre de Vesme, *Le Peintre-Graveur Italien*, Milan, 1906.

U.B.

28

MATTIA PRETI

Taverna (Calabria), 1613 – Malta, 1699

29 NUDE MAN WITH HIS HANDS TIED BEHIND HIM

VERSO: OLD MAN HOLDING A BOOK.

Red chalk, with traces of brown ink. 167 by 97 mm.; 6⅝ by 3¹³⁄₁₆ in.

PROVENANCE: A. Caselli (1968).

Because of his extensive travels and his varied artistic training, Mattia Preti never becomes the exclusive follower of any particular school. One of the most distinguished painters of the Neapolitan High Baroque, he responded to the influence of Guercino and Caravaggio in his early years when he visited Rome. During a stay in Venice in the early 1640s, he reacted to the work of Tintoretto and Veronese and became less Caravaggesque; when he returned to Rome in the early fifties, the Bolognese-Roman classicism of Guido Reni, Domenichino, and Sacchi became a major influence on his style. After returning to Naples in the late fifties, he finally settled in Malta in 1661 where he remained for most of his last years. His eclectic nature by no means diminished the power of his work, which is so often monumental in size and feeling.

The subject here is probably either the martyrdom of St. Sebastian or the flagellation of Christ. Preti's *St. Sebastian* in the Church of Santa Maria dei Sette Dolori, Naples, is typical of his several works on the subject, and is similar to the Bick drawing in the calm mood of the figure. Another figure, that of a Christ in a flagellation scene at S. Giovanni Calibita, Rome, also recalls the present drawing in its pose and serene stature.

Tomory (no. 47) draws a close comparison between the present drawing and a red chalk drawing by Preti of *Roman Charity* in the Ashmolean Museum (no. 926). Both are examples of Preti's typical use of wavy, sinuous line and soft parallel hatching to create form. The similar rendering of heads, especially in facial structure, is striking. Another analogous drawing, *A Demon with Two Putti* (*Cento Disegni Napoletani*, no. 81), shows Preti's characteristic hatching as well as this same rendering of the head. Although some of Preti's drawings have been connected with dated paintings, the development of his drawing style has not been sufficiently clarified to allow dating of the Bick drawing with any certainty.

The figure in the verso is possibly a St. Jerome. He is a nude, bald, older man and appears to carry a book in his right hand. This sketch is less finished than the drawing on the recto. Even lighter lines, perhaps Preti's first thoughts for the figure's pose, can be seen, particularly around the head.

BIBLIOGRAPHY: Aldo De Rinaldis, *Neapolitan Painting of the Seicento*, New York, 1929; Roberto Longhi, *Scritti Giovanili*, Florence, 1961; K. T. Parker, *Catalogue of the Collection of Drawings in the Ashmolean Museum*, Oxford, 1956; P. A. Tomory, *The Bick Collection of Italian Religious Drawings*, Sarasota, 1970; Walter Vitzthum, *Cento Disegni Napoletani*, Florence, 1967.

S.K.H.

29

CARLO MARATTI
Camerano, 1625 – Rome, 1713

30 HOLY FAMILY WITH ST. JOHN THE BAPTIST AND AN ANGEL

VERSO: THE HOLY FAMILY.

Red chalk. 230 by 262 mm.; 8$\frac{15}{16}$ by 10$\frac{5}{16}$ in.

Verso, in pen and brown ink, an illegible word.

PROVENANCE: E. Morrill; A. Vershbow.

Though not an innovator in seventeenth-century art, Carlo Maratti rivalled Gaulli and Pietro da Cortona as the artist of his day most popular with wealthy patrons, having worked on such huge projects as the Baptismal Chapel in St. Peter's, and the Altieri Palace, in Rome. His fresco and ceiling paintings are few, worked out after years of preparatory sketches for seemingly every detail, and then often executed by assistants. The Baptismal Chapel, for example, dragged on from 1692 until 1714, eight years after the master virtually stopped working, with help from his students, such as Passeri, Procaccini, and Chiari.

F. H. Dowley portrays Maratti as drawing from both major schools of the time, the classicism and strict draughtsmanship of Poussin, and the increasingly flamboyant and colorful baroque. A survey of his lively, but improbable, style of drapery is illustrative. In his outstanding catalogue, E. Schaar suggests four periods of development. The first is an apprenticeship looking to masters such as Raphael; the second is characterized by vigorous, angular, complex surfaces inspired by his teacher, Sacchi, and Guido Reni. Maratti's drapery of this period is almost self-supporting; Dowley paraphrases Maratti's own words on this subject: "while the nude derives all its form from nature, drapery has no natural form of its own, being totally dependent on the art and erudition of the artist for its *disegno*." Third, following the work of the more baroque Lanfranco, Maratti's line became softer, more harmonious and fluid, but at the same time, less decorative and more expressive of anatomy, that is, closer to the classical revival. Lastly, as Maratti's line became hard and brittle with age, his drapery once again became convoluted and free of the figure, though the influence of Mola made his figures more fluid. The development of Maratti's style, then, would be better described as a honing of the balance he found between the artistic forces of the period. This synthesis of calm monumentality and linear freshness was inspiration even to Goya (V. Sambricio, *Revue des Arts*, December, 1954).

Exact dates are difficult to fix with Maratti, as he was almost as painstaking and slow as Sacchi. Even a dated work, such as the Baptismal Chapel in St. Peter's, was in progress some years before, and after, the stated date. Dreyer, in his review of Schaar's work, has proposed that Schaar's dates of the periods of transition be advanced, so that the first period of independent development, to which the Bick drawing belongs, would begin about 1660; the transition to more melodious forms would occur about 1675; and the development of his final style would begin about 1685. Dr. Schaar has stated his opinion (by letter) that the Bick drawing is indeed

by Maratti and is from the 1670s, and, in final proof, cites a very similar print by Girolamo Frezza in the Bibliothèque Nationale, Paris, dated 1694, and inscribed as being designed by Maratti. Dr. Schaar notes that the Bick work is more finished than Maratti's usual preparations for his own paintings, as if it were indeed a model for a commission to be executed by a follower. Few artists have worked as closely and as extensively with their schools as Maratti.

The figures of this drawing are ideal types found in many Maratti compositions. A Madonna, Child, and attendant group, essentially the same as in this drawing, appears in several paintings; for example, the *Nativity*, 1651, Leningrad; *St. Philip Neri before the Virgin*, 1675, Palazzo Pitti, Florence; *Madonna with Sts. Carl and Ignatius*, 1685, S. M. in Vallicella, Rome; and a *Holy Family*, 1704, Kunsthistoriches Museum, Vienna. The Raby Castle collection of Lord Barnard, also, has a similar drawing, *Virgin Reading*.

BIBLIOGRAPHY: Francis H. Dowley, "Some Drawings by Carlo Maratti," *Burlington Magazine*, 1959, p. 65; F. H. Dowley, "Carlo Maratti, Carlo Fontana and the Baptismal Chapel in Saint Peter's," *Art Bulletin*, March, 1965; F. H. Dowley, "A Few Drawings by Carlo Maratti," *Master Drawings*, IV, 4, p. 422; Peter Dreyer, *Master Drawings*, Spring 1969, p. 172; A. Harris and E. Schaar, *Die Handzeichnungen von Andrea Sacchi und Carlo Maratti*, Düsseldorf, 1967; Hermann Voss, *Die Malerei des Barock in Rom*, Berlin, 1932.

P.C.S.

DOMENICO PIOLA

Genoa, 1627 – Genoa, 1703

31 FLIGHT INTO EGYPT

Pen and brown ink, brown bistre wash, some red chalk outlining. The sheet with the figures of the Virgin and Child and donkey has been pasted down in place of an earlier version of the subject. The upper left corner has been cropped and the whole drawing is laid down. 180 by 250 mm.; 7$\frac{1}{16}$ by 9$\frac{13}{16}$ in.

PROVENANCE: A Caselli (1968).

Born into the family of Genoese painters of the Casa Piola, Domenico first studied under the supervision of his brother, Pellagro (1617–40), and later in the workshop of Domenico Fiasella. Piola also worked in collaboration with Valerio Castello as his style reached maturity in the mid-fifties. The only extended period he was absent from his native city was in 1684–85 when he traveled to various north Italian cities to obtain commissions. Domenico had two sons whom he raised in the family tradition of painting and took with him on his journeys.

Mrs. Mary Newcome of the State University of New York at Binghamton has confirmed (orally) the attribution of the Bick drawing to Piola. She has dated it ca. 1650, and certainly not as late as 1655, when his compositions become more fluent, as in his preparatory study of that year in the Kunstmuseum, Düsseldorf, for an *Assumption of the Virgin*. The static composition of the Bick drawing is apparent when compared to Piola's later works; superfluous architecture interrupts any movement into space. Mrs. Newcome has also pointed out how close the Bick

work is to a drawing of the *Crucifixion*, also in Düsseldorf, which can be dated ca. 1650; the drawing is related to an unpublished painting, a *Rest on the Flight*, by Piola she has seen in a private collection in Genoa, as well as one in another private collection in Genoa (Malagoli, 1969, no. 97). The Flight into Egypt was a popular theme of the young Domenico. The figures of the Virgin and Child on the donkey have been added in place of the original grouping which had been carefully cut from the composition. The sunburst haloes of the Virgin and Child differ from the ring halo of Joseph. The wash employed in the added section is darker and more loosely applied, depending very little on line for the definition of forms.

The differences between the two sheets may be due to Domenico returning to the drawing at a later moment in his career to rethink its composition; another possibility is that the added sheet is by a student, perhaps his son Paolo Gerolamo.

BIBLIOGRAPHY: Keith Andrews, *Catalogue of Italian Drawings, National Gallery of Scotland*, Cambridge, 1968; Eloisa Malagoli, "The Drawings of Casa Piola," *Burlington Magazine*, CVIII, 1966; Eloisa Malagoli, *Mostra dei Pittori Genovesi a Genova*, Genoa, 1969.

G.K.S.

DOMENICO PERUZZINI

Pesaro, seventeenth century

32 THREE HEADS OF MEN

Black chalk, pen and brown ink; laid down. 220 by 154 mm.; 8 5/8 by 6 1/8 in.

Inscribed by the artist, in cartouche, top center, *Di Dom.co Peruzzini da Pesaro / Seg.re devotiss.o Ancona 21 Marzo / 1663*. Marks of the Hone Collection, Lugt 2793, and the Rogers Collection, Lugt 625.

PROVENANCE: Nathaniel Hone; C. Rogers; A. Caselli (1968).

Domenico Peruzzini, about whom little is known, was a printmaker and painter from Pesaro who worked in the middle of the seventeenth century. He studied under the religious painter G. G. Pandolfi and seems to have done much of his work in Ancona, although travels also took him to Alto, Rome, Bologna, Turin, and Milan.

The highly finished Bick drawing has all the feeling of a preliminary drawing for a print, evidently for a patron in Ancona, although Bartsch does not record a print of this subject in his catalogue of the artist's work. The subject seems to be the Three Ages of Man, a fairly common theme in Italian art. The style of this signed drawing, with its characteristic cross-hatching, is similar to other drawings which have been attributed to Peruzzini, for example, a landscape in Edinburgh (Andrews, RSA 342). Peruzzini's tight, vigorous definition of forms and "engraved" cross-hatching suggest a familiarity with draughtsmen and printmakers working in Florence in the early seventeenth century, such as Jacques Callot, Stefano della Bella (no. 27), Remigio Cantagallina (nos. 24, 25), and Ercole Bazzicaluva.

BIBLIOGRAPHY: Keith Andrews, *Catalogue of Italian Drawings, National Gallery of Scotland*, Cambridge, 1968; Adam Bartsch, *Le Peintre-Graveur*, XXI, Würzburg, 1920; Renato Roli, *I Disegni Italiani del Seicento*, Treviso, 1969.

G.K.S.

DE DOM. PERVZZINI DA PESARO
ae SEL denotiss. Ancona 15 Marzo
1663.

32

Follower of SALVATOR ROSA
Arenella, 1615 – Rome, 1673

33 MAN WITH A STAFF, TWO TREES, A MALE NUDE, THREE MALE HEADS AND THE HEAD OF A BEAR

Ink and oil paint, and brush, pen and black ink and black chalk added later; laid down. Condition: smudged, stained, edges torn. 250 by 213 mm.; 10 by 8 7/16 in. (irregular).

Inscribed in grey ink, *S. Rosa.*

PROVENANCE: W. Schatzki (1956).

This modest, tattered sheet is a unique opportunity for study, for it bears evidence of several of the many hands through which it has passed. The original artist, working with pen and light grey ink, sketched at least an outline of the beggar, and the tree, the head with ecclesiastic crown, the bound torso, the bear, and the fine heads at lower right. Some of the diagonal shading, the suggestion of terrain at lower right and Rosa's name were added in a darker grey ink, possibly by the same hand. Apparently another artist, using brown ink, traced the central figure and the best of the heads, and invented a second posture for the beggar. Highlights in yellow oil paint were added, and then, after the original sheet had been laid down on a piece of white paper, black chalk and ink, visible on the white paper through holes in the upper sheet. There seem to be, then, five separate stages of development.

The placing of soldiers and animals in Carraccesque landscapes is an invention of Rosa, the by-product of his early years spent as a bandit and wanderer in the mountainous north of Italy. The Bick drawing reminds one in particular of another drawing, *Figure of a Soldier in a Landscape* (Ozzola, fig. 3).

The followers of Rosa are so numerous that dating this drawing, even determining its century, is difficult. Rosa remained extremely popular from the unveiling of *Democritus* in the Pantheon in 1651 until his fiery, revolutionary landscapes thrilled Englishmen of the nineteenth century. This drawing approaches the style of Alessio de Marchis, a student of Rosa's landscapes, and also a Neapolitan, who worked in Rome, and then, after being imprisoned for burning a haystack in order to paint fires more realistically, primarily in Perugia, until 1752. The short, erratic strokes of wash seem foreign to de Marchis' interest in eerie lighting and broad, generalized composition, with the exception of his wildly impressionistic drawing *Shepherd in a Landscape*, in the Janos Scholz collection (Chiarini, 1967, p. 289).

One is also reminded, however, of Francesco Castiglione, the son and student of Rosa's great colleague, in the timid line and stability of the figures. There are several related artists of the eighteenth century as well, such as Zuccarelli in particular, and Fontebasso, for example, in some of the drawings attributed to them in the Albertina.

BIBLIOGRAPHY: Marco Chiarini, "Alessio de Marchis as a Draughtsman," *Master Drawings*, V, 3, 1967; Marco Chiarini, "Alcuni Quadri di paesaggio nel Museo di Belle Arti di Budapest," *Bulletin du Musée Hongrois des Beaux-Arts*, 32–33, 1969; Giuseppe Fiocco, *Disegni di una collezione veneziana del Settecento*, Venice, 1966; L. Ozzola, *Vita e Opere di Salvator Rosa*, Strassburg, 1908.

P.C.S.

33

FRA ANTONIO LORENZINI

Bologna, 1665 – Bologna, 1740

34 THE STORY OF JOSEPH, I

Red chalk; laid down. Vertical center fold. 363 by 518 mm.; 14 ¼ by 20 ⅞ in.

Bottom center inscribed by the artist, ANDREA DEL SARTO / FACIEBAT A V (A and V in monogram). Inscribed by a later hand, *A delsarto 15* . . . Marks of the Crozat Collection, Lugt 474; the Mariette Collection, Lugt 1872; an unidentified collection, Lugt 2694 or 2695.

PROVENANCE: P. J. Mariette; P. Crozat.

Gianantonio Lorenzini, known as Fra Antonio, was a Bolognese painter and engraver. A student of the Bolognese painter and printmaker Lorenzo Pasinelli, he turned very early in life to graphics. Lorenzini entered the Franciscan order where he continued to make prints after numerous artists, contemporary as well as old masters. In 1699 he was employed by the Grand Duke of Florence, Cosimo III, along with Verkruis, Mogalli, and other printmakers, to engrave a set of 147 plates after pictures in the ducal collection; among them were Andrea del Sarto's two paintings of the story of Joseph, now in the Pitti, the first of which has been copied precisely in the present drawing. This drawing shows various scenes from the early history of Joseph—Joseph recounting his dreams to his family, on the left, his departure for Shechem, his brothers conspiring against him, throwing him into the pit, and then selling him to the Ishmaelites, his coat being dipped in lamb's blood, and, finally, the coat being shown to Joseph's father.

P. A. Tomory (no. 30) has identified this drawing and a companion piece after Andrea's other painting of the story of Joseph, also in the Bick Collection, as Lorenzini's preparatory drawings for the prints commissioned by Cosimo III. Lorenzini's timid, stilted handling of the chalk, though far from the dramatic quality of the painting, or, indeed, of Andrea's own drawings (no. 1), is understandable in the preparation of a print, intended as a minutely exact copy of the painting, even down to the name and monogram. The painting itself was done by Andrea in 1515–16 for the decoration of a "camera di nozze" for Pier Francesco Borgherini and Margherita Acciauoli in the Casa Borgherini. It was sold by Giovanni Borgherini to the Grand Duke Francesco. In 1699 while working on the ducal collection, Lorenzini did the first known copy ever made of the painting.

BIBLIOGRAPHY: Adam Bartsch, *Le Peintre-Graveur*, XIX, Würzburg, 1920; Bryan, *Dictionary of Painters and Engravers*, London, 1904; Sidney J. Freedberg, *Andrea del Sarto*, Cambridge, 1963; P. A. Tomory, *The Bick Collection of Italian Religious Drawings*, Sarasota, 1970.

N.M.H.

34

RAPHAEL VRBINAS·
EXCVDEBAT·
M·

ALESSANDRO MAGNASCO

Genoa, 1677 – Genoa, 1749

35 SHEET OF STUDIES

Pen and brown ink, brown wash, black chalk, heightened with white. 295 by 425 mm.; 11 ½ by 16 ¾ in.

In pen and brown ink, upper left, *26*.

PROVENANCE: N. Chaikin (1964).

An outstanding feature of Magnasco's sketchbook drawings is the consistently fine figure relationships. The Bick drawing is one of the best of his compositions, for the three pairs of figures interrelate and create a tense and animated total composition. The fishermen pull their nets, which stretch diagonally across the page, toward the figures which focus around the tree; the tree, in turn, leans away from the center of the composition as if it were actually resisting the pull of the fishermen. The pair of figures reclining in the bottom center of the sheet repeat and reinforce the angle of the two outside figure groups and thus anchor the composition. A close look at the drawing reveals that the fishermen were originally sketched in the drawing further toward the center of the page. Similarly, faint chalk marks can be seen indicating that the slant of the tree was changed to its present position to pull against the fishermen. In addition, each individual figure forms three smaller and compositionally complete exercises.

Many of Magnasco's drawings have a number in the upper left hand corner. There are several drawings which carry the number *26* that appears on the Bick sheet. These include, besides the Bick drawing, (1) *Fishermen Resting and Woodsmen* in the Uffizi (Geiger, 1949, pl. 57); (2) *Two Women and a Man Running*, formerly collection of Benno Geiger (Geiger, 1949, pl. 467); (3) *Four Resting Figures*, Palazzo Bianco, Genoa (Morassi, fig. 127); (4) *Musicians*, Harvard University, Dumbarton Oaks; (5) *Travellers Resting*, in a New York private collection (Shickman, no. 19). The last of these is actually a pair of drawings, one of which has been pieced, with the number on a different sheet than the drawing, while the other has the number on a square patch pasted onto the drawing. Also, there are a number of drawings with numbers preceded by an *H*, for example, *H.io* inscribed in the upper left hand corner of *The Archangel Raphael and Tobias* in the Uffizi (Morassi, fig. 91). All the drawings with *H* and a number are religious. Possibly, the letter stands for the German word for holy or saint, "heilig." Since all the numbers appear to have been done by the same hand, it seems as though an early collector, perhaps German, arranged the drawings by subject and numbered them accordingly. Other numbered series seem to be tenuously connected by subject matter, especially the series marked *2*, which depicts almost exclusively hunters. The series in which the Bick drawing is included has less in common, having fishermen, travellers, woodsmen, musicians, and running figures; no general subject heading can be applied to all the drawings.

The figure group of the man, boy, and dog on the right of the page is directly related to a figure group in *Landscape with Figures* (Geiger, 1949, pl. 36).

35

BIBLIOGRAPHY: Benno Geiger, *I disegni del Magnasco*, Padua, 1945; Benno Geiger, *Magnasco*, Bergamo, 1949; Antonio Morassi, *Mostra del Magnasco*, Genoa, 1949; H. Shickman Gallery, *Catalogue of Old Master Drawings*, New York, 1966; J. B. Speed Art Museum and University of Michigan Museum of Art, *Alessandro Magnasco*, 1967, (cat. no. 29).

A.S.H.

PIER LEONE GHEZZI

Rome, 1674 – Rome, 1755

36 THE SIBYL OF CUMAE

Pen and brown ink, brown wash; vertical center fold. 274 by 186 mm.; 10¾ by 7⁵⁄₁₆ in.

Inscribed by the artist at the top, *La Sibilla di Cuma P L Ghezzi*; verso, in pencil, *A*.

PROVENANCE: W. Schatzki (1968).

It is ironic that this artist, who made his living as painter to Pope Clement XI and the Roman aristocracy, should be remembered for his hundreds of delightful caricatures. Ghezzi was a remarkably prolific man: he was a painter in oils and fresco, a printmaker, and a designer of festival architecture, tapestries, jewelry, and enamels. His caricatures must have been to some extent a leisurely occupation, a natural result of his wit and energy, and depict all the various strata of Roman society— tourists, low-life, and aristocracy.

Two styles of caricature may be differentiated in Ghezzi's work; the lovely nymphet of the Bick drawing is representative of the simpler, looser of the two. Other examples, inscribed by the same hand, are in the Museo Correr (*Arte Veneta*, fig. 363), the Museum of Fine Arts, Boston (Vitzhum, pl. 74), and in private collections (vom Prybam-Gladona, pl. 78). The other style, more highly finished and perhaps related to the artist's work as an etcher, is much better known and numerous examples exist, for example, in the Ashmolean (no. 1004), in the National Gallery of Scotland (RSA 132), and in the Albertina (nos. 838–907). Many of Ghezzi's caricatures were bought by English tourists (the British Museum has about 300 of them) and may have influenced caricaturists there (Fuchs, opp. p. 353).

Always unpretentious, sometimes obscene, caricature was a lively undergrowth of art and was particularly suited to the eighteenth century's refreshing irreverence. Like Ghezzi in Rome, Giovanni Battista Tiepolo drew many caricatures of all kinds of people, and this fascination with the grotesque and the peculiar honesty of the grotesque has a literary equivalent in the writings of Voltaire (notably *Candide*).

It is not surprising to find the artist caricaturing even the classical personages, in this case the Cumaean Sibyl. Although caricatures of other sibyls are not known to us, a drawing in the Julius Held collection (no. 123) presents a younger, slimmer version of Dr. Bick's sibyl and is identified by the artist at the top of the sheet as the Cyprian Venus.

La Sibilla di Cuma — P.L. Ghezzi

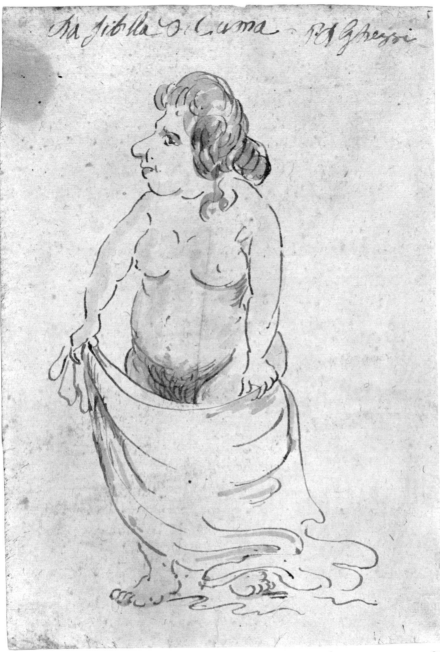

36

BIBLIOGRAPHY: Keith Andrews, *National Gallery of Scotland, Catalogue of the Italian Drawings*, Cambridge, 1968; *Arte Veneta*, XXI, 1967; Anthony Blunt and Edward Croft-Murray, *Venetian Drawings of the XVII and XVIII Centuries . . . at Windsor Castle*, London, 1957; Eduard Fuchs, *Die Frau in der Karikatur*, Munich, 1907; Julius Held, *Selections from the Drawing Collection of Mr. and Mrs. Julius Held*, Binghamton, 1970; W. R. Juynboll, *Het Komische Genre in de Italiaansche Schilderkunst gedurende de Zeventiende en de Achttiende Eeuw*, 1934; M. Loret, "Pier Leone Ghezzi," *Capitolium*, XI, 1935; K. T. Parker, *Catalogue of the Collection of Drawings in the Ashmolean Museum*, II, Oxford, 1956; Charlotte vom Prybam-Gladona, *Unbekannte Zeichnungen alter Meister aus europäischen Privatbesitz*, Munich, 1969; Alfred Stix and L. Fröhlich-Bum, *Beschreibender Katalog der Handzeichnungen*, III, Vienna, 1932; W. Vitzhum, *A Collection of Italian Drawings from North American Collections*, Montreal, 1970.

J.A.W.

Attributed to MARCO RICCI

Belluno, 1676 – Venice, 1730

37 STAGE DESIGN: LANDSCAPE WITH RUINS AND CLASSICAL STATUES

Pen and brown ink, brown wash, touches of black chalk, border in black ink; laid down. 260 by 365 mm.; 10 ¼ by 14 ⅞₆ in.

Inscribed by the artist with numbers from one through six, eight and nine, and right center, *alto 7 Piedi*. Mark of the Mayor Collection, Lugt 2799.

PROVENANCE: W. Mayor; A. Mathews (1964).

Marco Ricci was an important eighteenth-century landscape painter and printmaker. He worked in various cities in Italy, and in London on two separate occasions: from 1708 to 1710 or 1711 with Giovanni Antonio Pellegrini and, after a brief return to Venice, again from 1712 to 1716 with his uncle Sebastiano Ricci.

The present drawing is particularly characteristic of Ricci in its emphasis on classical ruins, which appear very often in his drawings, tempera panels (Buckingham Palace, no. 146959), and etchings (Pittaluga, figs. 25, 26). Certain rather loose pen-and-ink and wash drawings very like the Bick drawing in character contain the same statues and architecture. For example, a work in the Louvre (*Commentari*, fig. 11) is spatially composed very similarly and contains the composition of the statue of Cleopatra framed by columns and cornice. Another view of this statue is in the Ashmolean (Pilo, fig. 166) and the background trees there are very close to those in the Bick drawing. An equestrian statue and the Arch of Titus appear also in a *Landscape with Ruins* (Pilo, fig. 165).

The drawing is clearly a preparatory study for a stage set. The numerical annotation is rather unusual and denotes the wings and back shutter on which the scene was to have been painted; wings and shutters were canvas flats on wooden frames which slid horizontally on and off stage to effect a scene change. Numbers one and two denote those elements that would have been painted on the first two pairs of

wings, respectively; behind these in order were single wings numbered three, four, five, six, and eight (seven is curiously missing), and nine was the shutter which closed the rear of the scene. The height of the archway is given as seven feet. Not shown are the stock borders of clouds which hid the stage ceiling from audience view. The wings of this set were to be cut out in profile on their inside edges, and wings number five, the statue of Cleopatra, number six, the equestrian statue, and number eight, the pyramid of Cestius, would have been freestanding "cut-scenes" which have been common since the seventeenth century (Southern, pp. 145–146). By this time, asymmetrical operatic sets with vanishing points to the far left or right were not unusual (Scholz, figs. 24, 25, 26).

One is tempted to assign this drawing to one of Ricci's sojourns in London, where he achieved some renown as a designer of operas at the Opera House in Haymarket —in fact, he seems to be the first scene designer to receive credit in the text or bill of a play (Nicoll, p. 34). Although it is unclear which productions Ricci designed, some twenty were produced at the Opera House between 1708 and 1716 (a witness to the popularity of the newly imported Italian opera among the British aristocracy). The difficulty with such an identification is that the set depicted would have been too deep for the typical English stage of the period, which accommodated normally no more than five pairs of wings. However, very little is known about the stage at the Opera House, which was built in 1705 and remodeled several times. Moreover, the shallow English stage was sometimes deepened especially for opera (cf. Southern, pp. 177–193). Theatres of the required depth were common on the continent, and Ricci may certainly have designed sets there as well as in London.

The ruin motif in stage design had been known in England from the time of Inigo Jones's court masques of a century before (Strong, fig. 19).

BIBLIOGRAPHY: Michael Milkovich, *Sebastiano and Marco Ricci in America*, Lexington (Kentucky), 1966; Allardyce Nicoll, *A History of the Early Eighteenth Century Drama 1700–1750*, Cambridge, 1925; O. F. Osti, "In Margine alla Mostra di Belluno: Marco Ricci," *Commentari*, VI, 1956; G. M. Pilo, *Marco Ricci—Catalogo della Mostra*, Venice, 1963; Mary Pittaluga, *Acquafortisti Veneziani del Settecento*, Florence, 1952; János Scholz, *Baroque and Romantic Stage Design*, New York, 1962; Richard Southern, *Changeable Scenery—Its Origin and Development in the British Theatre*, London, 1952; Ray Strong, *Festival Designs by Inigo Jones*, Chatsworth, 1966.

J.A.W.

GIOVANNI BATTISTA PIAZZETTA
Venice, 1682 – Venice, 1754

38 BOY WITH A LUTE

Black chalk heightened with white. 363 by 294 mm.; 14⅜ by 11⁹⁄₁₆ in.

Mark of the Beurdeley Collection, Lugt 421. Verso, printed label, *174*; in pencil, *Piazzetta*.

PROVENANCE: A. Beurdeley; a German collection; N. Chaikin (1965).

Giovanni Battista Piazzetta, the son of a woodcarver, first trained under his father, but at an early age he abandoned his first medium and became the pupil of the painter Antonio Molinari. When he was twenty Piazzetta left Venice for Bologna where he studied under Giuseppe Maria Crespi, whose concern with heavy forms, sharp contrasts of light and shadow, and genre scenes were an important factor in Piazzetta's development. Among his followers were Domenico Maggiotto (no. 42), Francesco Cappella, Egidio Dall'Olio, and Giuseppe Angeli, and he deeply influenced Giambattista Tiepolo, the greatest painter of eighteenth-century Venice.

Piazzetta's works fall into two main divisions: religious and genre. Patrons who commissioned religious works for altarpieces often retained genre pieces for their private collections. A large category of the genre pieces includes heads, painted or drawn, and the present drawing is one of these. Unlike the witty, everyday scenes portrayed in the genre painting of contemporary artists like Pietro Longhi, Piazzetta's genre works combine fantasy and reality, achieving an almost classical weight. His subjects are often drawn wearing exotic costume, but they retain a realistic humanity in their portrayal.

The same sitter as the boy with the lute in the Bick drawing is seen again in the portrait of a boy and a dog at Windsor Castle attributed to Piazzetta (Blunt, pl. 10, cat. no. 55). The awkwardness of the composition of the Windsor drawing suggests that perhaps it is a copy of the Bick drawing. The face, hair, and pose in both drawings are essentially the same, but the substitution of the clumsily executed dog for the lute unbalances the composition. The Bick drawing is handsome in its simplicity. The lute and the line of the boy's arm and head form neatly opposing diagonals. The clothes of the boy in the Windsor drawing are bulky and awkward in comparison to the same details in the Bick drawing. The Windsor drawing could be a copy of the Bick drawing by the master himself or, more likely, by one of his students; it is common for copyists to keep the actual pose of a figure but change the reason for the pose, thus disguising their borrowing at the expense of the spontaneity and naturalness of the original composition.

It is difficult to arrange Piazzetta's drawings in any chronological order by their stylistic development. Blunt places the Windsor drawings similar to the Bick work at about 1735.

BIBLIOGRAPHY: Anthony Blunt, *Venetian Drawings of the XVII and XVIII Centuries in the Collection of Her Majesty the Queen at Windsor Castle*, London, 1957; Rodolfo Palluchini, *La Pittura Veneziana del Settecento*, Venice, 1965; Rodolfo Pallucchini, *Piazzetta*, Milan, 1956; Leona E. Prasse, "A Portrait Drawing by Piazzetta," *Cleveland Museum of Art Bulletin*, January, 1935, pp. 3–4; Leona E. Prasse, "Five Portrait Drawings by Piazzetta," *Cleveland Museum of Art Bulletin*, April, 1931, pp. 73–76.

A.S.H.

Giovanni Battista Piazzetta
38 BOY WITH A LUTE

GASPARE DIZIANI

Belluno, 1689 – Venice, 1767

39 THE REST ON THE FLIGHT INTO EGYPT

Red chalk, pen and brown ink. 257 by 352 mm.; 10 1/8 by 13 7/8 in.

PROVENANCE: A. L. de Mestral de Saint Saphorin; R. de Cérenville; N. Chaikin.

Gaspare Diziani first studied under Gregorio Lazzarini; the most important influence on the young Diziani was the painting of the great Venetian, Sebastiano Ricci. During his stays in Munich and Dresden, from 1712 to 1717, Gaspare worked as a stage designer in the Court of Saxony where he created many paintings and theatre decorations. His greatest work, though, was done in Venice, where he was the founder of the Accademia, of which he was elected President in 1760 and 1766.

Differentiating the works of Diziani, Fontebasso, and Pellegrini still troubles art historians, and this uncertainty prevents a final attribution of the Bick drawing. In format, the present drawing is very similar to a drawing of the *Storm at Sea* in the Albertina (no. 336), which is attributed to Fontebasso. In both works, the main figures occupy the foreground, two or three cherubs oversee the scene, and, instead of a middle-ground, the distant background stands directly behind the foreground figures. The abbreviated sweeps of line in the Albertina drawing, though, differ from the nervously angular strokes in the Bick drawing. In pen style the present drawing is also very similar to a drawing of the *Annunciation* attributed to Diziani, in the Museo Correr (Ojetti, pl. 171).

In subject and format, the Bick drawing may be related to a fresco by Diziani in San Stefano in Venice (Coletti, fig. 1), showing the Holy Family in their flight into Egypt. Although the fresco and the preparatory drawings for it in the Museo Correr and the Janos Scholz collection show the group moving from left to right, the arrangement, almost a cascade, of people, angels, and animals to the edge of the sheet, parallel to the picture plane, the spontaneity of the defintion of the figures, and the beautiful way the artist plays the two media against each other suggest that the Bick drawing may have been one step in the artist's thinking about this commission. Gaspare's son, Giuseppe Diziani, was also a draughtsman whose works sometimes seem to have captured much of the boldness of his father's productions.

BIBLIOGRAPHY: Luigi Coletti, "Affreschi di Gaspare Diziani," *Bollettino d'Arte*, XXVIII, 1935; Ugo Ojetti, *Il Settecento Italiano*, Rome, 1932; Terisio Pignatti, *Disegni veneti del settecento nel Museo Correr di Venezia*, Venice, 1964; Alfred Stix and L. Fröhlich-Bum, *Beschreibender Katalog der Handzeichnungen*, I, Vienna, 1926.

G.K.S.

GIOVANNI BATTISTA TIEPOLO
Venice, 1696 – Madrid, 1770

40 STANDING FIGURE

Red chalk, heightened with white, on buff paper. Watermark: three circles, one on top of the other, surmounted by a cross. 336 by 150 mm.; 14½ by 5¹⁵⁄₁₆ in. (irregular).

Verso, in pencil, *No. 4.*

PROVENANCE: A. L. de Mestral de Saint Saphorin; R. de Cérenville; N. Chaikin (1968).

As George Knox has pointed out (by letter), this rapid, extremely fluent drawing is a study by Giambattista for a figure in the ceiling fresco of the Throne Room in Madrid (Molmenti, p. 192). Since the figure does not appear in the oil sketch in Washington (Morassi, pl. 79), our drawing must date from the actual painting of the fresco, 1762–64.

The fresco, *The Apotheosis of Spain*, was the main element in Tiepolo's decoration of Charles II's new palace. It depicts Spain enthroned in a vast sky, surrounded by the floating figures of virtues and vices, angels, putti, and ancient gods. Around the edges, just above the cornice of the room, figures in contemporary dress stand on an illusionistic ledge in front of a painted cornice that meets the sky. Our drawing is one of these figures, representing the provinces of Spain and the regions of the world, which provide a visual and psychological bridge between the viewer below and the allegorical groups in the sky (Morassi, pls. 82–90).

Our drawing comes from the collection of Armand Louis de Mestral de Saint Saphorin (1738–1806), Danish Ambassador to the courts of Poland, Spain, Holland, Russia, and Austria-Hungary, who acquired a large number of drawings directly from the Tiepolo studio in Venice. These eventually entered the private collection of René de Cérenville in Switzerland, where they remained until his death in 1968.

BIBLIOGRAPHY: George Knox, *Catalogue of the Tiepolo Drawings in the Victoria and Albert Museum*, London, 1960; George Knox, *Tiepolo, A Bicentenary Exhibition*, Harvard University, 1970; Pompeo Molmenti, *G. B. Tiepolo: La sua vita e le sue opere*, Milan, 1909; Antonio Morassi, *G. B. Tiepolo: His Life and Work*, London, 1955.

J.G.F.

GIAN BATTISTA CROSATO
Venice, 1679 – Venice, 1758

41 TWO ANGELS AND TWO PUTTI

Pen and brown ink, grey wash, black chalk; laid down. 192 by 132 mm.; 7⁹⁄₁₆ by 5⁵⁄₁₆ in. (irregular).

40

Overlapping the drawing and the mat, two unidentified collector's marks, Lugt 486b and 2079b (C. Argenteri and P. G. Breschi?). On the mat, in pen and brown ink, *Sante Varni* (see Lugt 987a); two words in pen and brown ink erased; in pencil, *G. A. Pellegrini 1675 – 1741, PC+*, and *7*.

PROVENANCE: Santevarni; C. Argenteri (?); P. G. Breschi (?); Alister Mathews (1965).

Gian Battista Crosato followed in the tradition of the elaborate, light and airy style of the Italian Rococo. His major works are richly decorative frescoes depicting largely mythological and allegorical subject matter, as in his frescoes in Stupinigi, as well as in the stage designs he undertook (Viale-Ferrero, pl. XI). His colors are crystal clear and warm, his forms full-blown and rich. His masterpiece, *Allegory of the Four Parts of the World* (Palluchini, figs. 75, 76), embellishes the ceiling of the *sala di ballo* of the Ca' Rezzonico in Venice.

Two Angels and Two Putti is typical of the figure groups Crosato employed in his paintings and drawings. It is closely related stylistically to *Zephyr and Flora* in the Museo Correr (Pignatti, no. 15). Both drawings are lithe and spontaneous, in striking contrast to *St. Charles Borromaeus Distributing Alms* (Seilern, no. 127), which is characterized by heavier, tighter forms and large areas of darker wash. The Correr and Bick drawings in particular accord well with the style of the Stupinigi frescoes from the earlier part of Crosato's career.

The composition of the Bick drawing, two-dimensionally, is organized along a grid-pattern. The right arm of the highest angel points to the upper left corner of the composition and its line is carried down through the angel's leg which extends toward the lower right portion of the drawing. This diagonal is parallel to the slant of the second angel's head, torso, and right leg. The putto at the bottom of this composition repeats the same slope again. The opposing diagonal is formed by the line running from the second angel's arms which point to the left side of the sheet to the skillfully foreshortened left hand of the uppermost angel. This line is reinforced by the wash and repeated in the angle of the higher putto. All these slanting lines intersect along the near vertical midline of the composition. Viewed three-dimensionally, the composition is the traditional upward spiral of the Rococo, starting at the lower putto's left foot and winding upward to the right hand of the highest figure.

The chain and wire lines formed in the production of the rag paper show that the artist originally may have intended the orientation of the figures within the rectangle of the sheet (now of irregular shape) to be such that the right hand of the upper angel would be even more the pinnacle of the composition and the whole figure slightly more vertical. This orientation would also place the upper angel's head directly above the lowest point in the drawing, the lower putto's left foot. Crosato based the composition of a large portion of his work on this nearly regular diamond grid pattern. It is more obvious in his drawing *Zephyr and Flora*, and can be seen clearly in another of his pen drawings, *Madonna in Glory* (Pignatti, no. 81). His frescoes are also loosely organized on this simple spiral or grid pattern.

N.º 26. Collezione Paolo Vanni

BIBLIOGRAPHY: Alessandro Bettagno, *Una collezione veneziana del Settecento*, Venice, 1966; Giuseppe Fiocco, *Giambattista Crosato*, Venice, 1941; Antoine Seilern, *Italian Paintings and Drawings at 56 Princes Gate London SW 7*, London, 1959; Rodolfo Palluchini, *La Pittura Veneziana del Settecento*, Venice, 1965; Terisio Pignatti, *Disegni veneti del Settecento nel Museo Correr di Venezia*, Venice, 1964; Mercedes Viale-Ferrero, *La scenografia del '700 e i fratelli Galliari*, Turin, 1964.

A.S.H.

DOMENICO MAGGIOTTO
Venice, 1713 – Venice, 1793

42 PORTRAIT OF A YOUNG SCULPTOR

Black and white chalk. 354 by 272 mm.; 13 15/16 by 10 3/4 in.

Verso, in pencil, *Piazzetta / ehemals Privatbesitz Puppel-Berlin*; various modern inventory numbers.

PROVENANCE: Puppel; W. Schatzki (1967).

Domenico Maggiotto is one of several close followers of the great Venetian master Giovanni Battista Piazzetta (no. 38); little is known of the careers of these artists and their several styles have not been differentiated. For example, it is difficult to be sure whether this fine drawing is by Maggiotto or Egidio dall'Olio or Francesco Capella, and its slightly rubbed condition adds to the problem. However, we see here an authentic example of Piazzetta's direct influence, with its concentration on the massive volumes of the bust and one hand of a figure, here a youth dressed in the fur-trimmed coat that appears in several paintings and drawings by Piazzetta himself. The gap between this school piece and an imitation by a much later hand may be seen in two drawings of precisely similar subject in the Fogg Museum (nos. 166, 167), one of them by Piazzetta and the other by a much weaker artist.

An example of the confusing problem of separating Piazzetta's work from that of his students, and also of determining which student authored each piece, can be seen in studying four clearly related genre portraits. *A Bust of a Young Girl* (Collobi, pl. 116) and a *Bust of a Boy With a Violin* (Collobi, pl. 117), both attributed to Maggiotto, are strikingly similar to another portrait pair also attributed to this artist formerly in the art market, New York (Shickman, pls. 47, 48), although there the boy on the right is holding a money bag instead of a violin. The hair, clothes, and pose of the two female portraits are almost identical. Another bust of a girl attributed to Piazzetta in the Art Museum, Princeton (*Mower*, pl. 33), further complicates the problem; the high quality of the Princeton drawing suggests that it may be by the master himself and, perhaps, the original for the other versions.

BIBLIOGRAPHY: Licia Ragghianti Collobi, *Disegni della Fondazione Horne in Firenze*, Florence, 1963; Agnes Mongan and Paul J. Sachs, *Drawings in the Fogg Museum of Art*, Cambridge, Mass., 1940; *The Elsa Durand Mower Collection of French and Italian Drawings*, Princeton University, 1968; Terisio Pignatti, *Disegni veneti del Settecento nel Museo Correr di Venezia*, Venice, 1964; H. Shickman Gallery, *Exhibition of Old Master Drawings*, New York, 1966.

A.S.H.

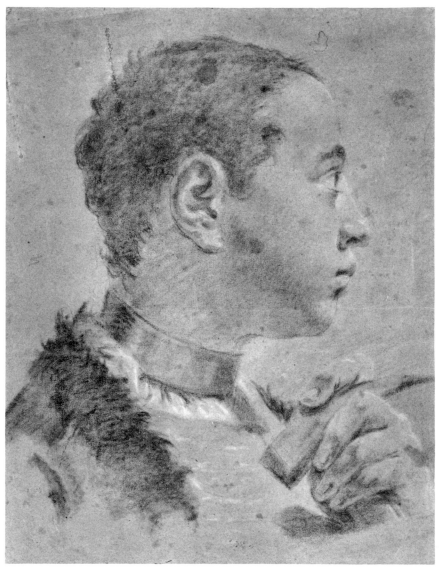

42

DOMENICO TIEPOLO
Venice, 1727 – Venice, 1804

43 HEAD OF A BOY

Black chalk, heightened with white chalk, on blue-grey paper; laid down. Water stain upper right. 223 by 173 mm.; 8¾ by 6¾ in.

On the verso, visible from the recto, are an old number and price, in brown ink, typical of the drawings at Stuttgart.

PROVENANCE: according to an old notation, Stuttgarter Kunstkabinett (no. 20); Sotheby's, July 13, 19...; H. Swetzoff (1955).

Most of Domenico's chalk drawings date from the first half of his career, and are difficult to distinguish from those of his father and teacher, Giambattista. On stylistic grounds, this drawing seems to belong to the son; it exhibits the hesitant line and careful modeling of Domenico's early work.

Apprentices in the Tiepolo studio often made drawings after paintings and frescoes. Stylistic comparisons might suggest this type of drawing (Knox, 1968, pls. 52–55); however, the Bick drawing evidently does not correspond precisely to any painted head by Giambattista. On the other hand, the drawing could be a preparatory study for the head of the acolyte at the right in Domenico's *soppraporta* at Würzburg of Saint Ambrose (Molmenti, p. 63). However, a study of Domenico for the hands of Saint Ambrose in the Museo Correr (Lorenzetti, pl. 13v), with its rapid, agitated strokes, differs greatly from ours, although this may simply reflect the difference in dramatic content of the two figures.

George Knox has convincingly suggested that this is a drawing by Domenico of his younger brother Lorenzo. In this case, it would be an independent sketch; it is not a preparatory study for any of the portraits of Lorenzo that have been identified in various paintings (Shaw, pl. 54, notes). Chalk studies in the Museo Correr of a boy asleep, inscribed *Loren*, are attributed by Pignatti to Domenico (Pignatti, no. 108); our drawing may be of similar origin. The youthful look of the sitter, who was born in 1736, indicates roughly the Würzburg period, ca. 1750, or earlier. Stylistically, the handling of chalk is similar to drawings after the Scalzi fresco of 1745 (Knox, 1968).

The numbering on the verso, from the late eighteenth or early nineteenth century, indicates a serial number and price probably connected with an early sale; these notations, common to many drawings from the Tiepolo circle, have been discussed at length by Knox (Knox, Stuttgart, p. 8).

BIBLIOGRAPHY: George Knox, "G. B. Tiepolo and the Ceiling of the Scalzi," *Burlington Magazine*, July, 1968; George Knox, *Tiepolo*, Stuttgart, 1970; George Knox, *Tiepolo, a Bicentenary Exhibition*, Harvard University, 1970; Giulio Lorenzetti, *Il Quaderno dei Tiepoli al Museo Correr di Venezia*, Venice, 1946; Terisio Pignatti, *Disegni Veneti del Settecento nel Museo Correr di Venezia*, Venice, 1964; James Byam Shaw, *The Drawings of Domenico Tiepolo*, London, 1962.

J.G.F.

43

UBALDO GANDOLFI

San Matteo, 1728 – Ravenna, 1787

44 THE APOTHEOSIS OF SAN VITALE

Pen and brown ink, grey wash, black chalk. 266 by 224 mm.; 10 7/16 by 8 3/4 in.

Unidentified collector's mark in blue diamond (with G or C and M?), three times (in corners); unidentified mark (M?); in pencil, *366* (in circle); indecipherable words in pencil. Verso, in pen and brown ink, *Ubaldo Gandolfi Pensiere per la Cupola di S. Vitale di Ravenna*; in pen and brown ink, *231 VC* (in monogram); *H. 121*; unidentified collector's mark in blue; mark of the Morassi collection, Lugt 143a; in pencil, *chiesa destrutta bombe austriache 1917* . . . (the church in Ravenna actually destroyed was S. Apollinare Nuovo and the correct date is 1916); in pencil, *Unico documento autentico e originale*; in pencil, *366* (crossed out); *46a, 26.3 × 22.2 cm.*

PROVENANCE: A. Morassi; Mewes Collection, Paris; Colnaghi; N. Chaikin (1968).

The Apotheosis of San Vitale is a study for the fresco in San Vitale in Ravenna started in 1780 by the Bolognese artist, Ubaldo Gandolfi, and finished after his death by Giacomo Guarana. Along with the *Glorification of San Vitale* (Held catalogue, pl. 122), this beautiful drawing, typical of the brilliant assurance of this master, is part of a chronological sequence culminating in the fine fresco for this Byzantine church, better known today for its famous sixth-century mosaics. In spite of the slight differences in size, the Bick and the Held sheets might still be from the same notebook, not only because of similarities of style and medium and the fact they are studies for the same project, but also because they both have a vertical fold along the left edge (in the case of the Bick drawing, at least, the fold appears to have been reinforced with black chalk).

The Bick drawing is a more powerful composition, leading from the lower left portion to the upper right diagonally across the cupola. The figures are more distinctly worked out and the wash is more carefully controlled than in the Held drawing, indicating that the Bick drawing is perhaps a later and more careful study for the final fresco.

A copy of a preliminary sketch for the cupola (Ricci, p. 278) shows an intermediary stage between the Bick drawing and the final fresco, and also seems to support the theory that the Bick drawing is a reworking of the Held drawing. In this, S. Vitale is moved from the central position he holds in the Bick study and is placed slightly higher and to the right. His pose is changed; he holds the banner himself and has changed the direction of his gaze toward the source of light, the upper left hand portion, as in the Bick drawing. S. Benedetto, Ravenna's other patron saint, is included in the composition. He too looks toward the upper left. Along with the angel which breaks the frame of the oculus in a baroque manner, S. Vitale and S. Benedetto form a strong diagonal from the lower left to the upper right.

The final composition as it appears in the fresco is more stable and balanced than any of the preliminary sketches. The angel breaking the frame of the oculus has

44

moved to the lower right-hand portion below S. Vitale, reinforcing the opposing diagonal formed by the stream of light emanating from the upper left and shining down between the two saints. This composition with its intersecting diagonals forms a stable triangle within the oculus.

In the Bick drawing, S. Vitale is supported and emphasized by a tangle of angels and putti half-obscured in the clouds. In the fresco this composition is refined and simplified, leaving only one angel who is spatially in front of the saint, making him distinct. The number of putti has been reduced, and they are also no longer lost in the composition as they are in the Bick drawing.

BIBLIOGRAPHY: Lidia Bianchi, *I Gandolfi*, Rome, 1968; *Burlington Magazine*, CX, April, 1968, p. lxxxi; Corrado Ricci, "Le Pitture della Cupola di S. Vitale in Ravenna," *Cronache d'Arte*, July–August, 1927; *Selections from the Drawing Collection of Mr. and Mrs. Julius S. Held*, Binghamton, 1970.

A.S.H.

PIETRO GIACOMO PALMIERI
Bologna, 1737 – Turin, 1804

45 LANDSCAPE

Pen and black ink. Watermark: fleur-de-lis surmounting a shield with a diagonal bar. 240 by 360 mm.; 9 ½ by 13 ¹⁵⁄₁₆ in.

Inscribed by the artist, lower center, *P. Palmerius Invenit, et Fecit 1774.*

PROVENANCE: H. Swetzoff (1958).

Pietro Giacomo Palmieri studied in Bologna under Ercole Graziani il Giovane (1688–1765, a student of Donati Creti). Confusion between the father Pietro Giacomo and the son Pietro Giovanni (1780–1855, at Turin) arises because of the similarity of name. Further consideration needs also to be given to Giovanni Battista (1674–1740), Pietro Giacomo's father, who worked in Genoa, and to Francesco Palmieri, who is listed on the records of the Accademia Clementina as drawing master in Bologna, 1782 (Delogu, p. 385).

Pietro Giacomo Palmieri's earliest work was included in a series of prints published by Guidotti in 1760. He is known to have traveled to Paris (1771–79) where he made the Bick drawing, dated 1774, and briefly to other northern countries. Palmieri is recorded as a member of the Academies at Bologna and Parma. He went to Turin and worked there, until his death, as drawing master of the university and for Prince Luigi di Carignano and Vittorio Amadeo III. Baudi di Vesme, in 1884, records receiving from Palmieri's granddaughter a manuscript biography of the artist by Giuseppe Francesco Regis.

This landscape is a clear example of Palmieri's work imitative of well-known masters but with no intention of deception, e.g., two trompe l'oeil drawings by Palmieri in the Metropolitan Museum of New York and a similar "folio" drawing in Turin (Bertini, no. 661), where he directly represents signed drawings and engravings by such artists as Guercino, Stefano della Bella, and Karel Dujardin. Also

in Turin (Bertini, no. 667: I and II) are two drawings of beggars signed "Sig. Palmieri Figlio" that are copied from works by Jacques Callot; apparently, Pietro Giacomo's son imitated old masters as well.

The present drawing, done in the manner of Guercino, is characterized by a fluent and energetic rococo line. Another landscape drawing signed by Palmieri at the British Museum shows this same French rococo style, similar to Claude Joseph Vernet. A pen-and-wash drawing at the British Museum has the same setting as the Bick drawing but with figure and cattle departing towards the right. The Bick drawing may have been a preparatory study for a print.

Palmieri's landscapes are recorded as popular among French aristocrats of the time; P. G. Wille writes in his journal of January, 1775, "M. Palmieri, Italien, m'a fait deux dessins, un peu dans le goût du Guerchin. Je les lui ay payés un louis pièce." The similarity of this drawing and especially Palmieri's wash drawings (Ashmolean, no. 1030) to the work of Nicolaes Berchem (1620–83) is significant. A series of followers of Berchem in Paris in the late Settecento is mentioned by Hollstein, e.g., J. J. de Boissieu, P. Aveline, P. A. Martini, and M. Pacini. A northern Italian, Domenico Pecchio (at Verona), made direct copies of Berchem etchings in the 1700s, confirming a purely Italian interest in Berchem's style.

BIBLIOGRAPHY: Aldo Bertini, *I Disegni Italiani Della Biblioteca Reale di Torino*, Rome, 1958; Giuseppe Delogu, "Pietro Giacomo Palmieri," *Pantheon*, December, 1935; Joseph Meder, *Die Handzeichnung*, Vienna, 1923; Agnes Mongan and Paul J. Sachs, *Drawings in the Fogg Museum of Art*, Cambridge, 1940; K. T. Parker, *Catalogue of the Collection of Drawings in the Ashmolean Museum*, Oxford, 1956; J. G. Wille, *Mémoires et Journal de Wille*, Paris, 1857.

S.K.H.

Anonymous Italian, eighteenth century

46 VIEW OF THE CASTEL SANT'ANGELO FROM THE BANK OF THE TIBER

Pen and brown ink, black chalk, grey washes. Repaired in lower left and lower right corners. Watermark: *VI* or *IV*. Image: 300 by 382 mm.; 11¹³⁄₁₆ by 15 in. Paper: 329 by 427 mm.; 13 by 16⅞ in.

PROVENANCE: C. R. Rudolph; A. Mathews (1959).

The Castel Sant'Angelo, dominating the northwestern quarter of Rome, had been a much drawn and painted view from the late sixteenth century on (Krönig, pp. 385–417). The Bick drawing is suggestive of similar views by Gaspar van Wittel (Gaspare Vanvitelli, 1653–1736), whose paintings and drawings of the subject are numerous (Briganti, figs. 83–91, 176d, 188d). However, he never portrayed the precise same view, and an examination of details in the Bick drawing and several Vanvitelli's, particularly the vegetation, make that attribution doubtful (Briganti, 197d). Other reasonable possibilities are an artist from the circle of Canaletto (Canaletto himself worked in Rome and painted a view of the Castel Sant'Angelo, Krönig, fig. 283), or perhaps Isaac de Moucheron (1667–1744), a Dutchman who

also used the Castel as subject (*Zeichner Sehen die Antike*, fig. 51). The possibility that the Bick drawing was done by a foreigner, perhaps French or Dutch, cannot be discounted.

Certainly not a sketch, this highly finished drawing was doubtless meant to be sold, perhaps to the English amateur collectors who became so numerous on the Continent in the eighteenth century.

The horizon line is lightly drawn in black chalk across the page and terminated by a pin prick at either end.

BIBLIOGRAPHY: Giuliano Briganti, *Gaspar Van Wittel e l'origine della veduta settecentesca*, Rome, 1966; Wolfgang Krönig, "Geschichte Einer Rom-Vedute," *Miscellanea Bibliothecae Hertzianae*, Munich, 1961; Mattias Winner, *Zeichner Sehen die Antike-Europäische Handzeichnungen 1450–1800*, Berlin-Dahlem, 1967.

J.A.W.

Index of Artists

SET IN TYPE BY THE STINEHOUR PRESS

PRINTED BY THE MERIDEN GRAVURE COMPANY